OPPORTUNITIES IN COMPUTER SCIENCE CAREERS

Julie Lepick Kling

VGM Career Horizons
A Division of National Textbook Company
4255 West Touhy Avenue
Lincolnwood, Illinois 60646-1975 U.S.A.

Photo Credits
Front cover: upper left, Burroughs Corporation; upper right, IBM
Corporation; lower left, DeVRY, INC.; lower right, NTC stock.
Back cover: upper left, NTC stock; upper right, Texas Instruments Data
Systems Group; lower left, Gould, Inc.; lower right, Texas Instruments Data
Systems Group.

ABOUT THE AUTHOR

Julie Lepick Kling is a technical writer specializing in the computer field. Currently a member of the documentation staff at Data General in Westboro, Massachusetts, she has also taught graduate and undergraduate courses in technical communication at Texas A&M University and at California State University, Long Beach. The recipient of numerous awards and grants, Dr. Kling has published many scholarly and journalistic articles and reviews and presented papers at conferences throughout the U.S. She has worked as a consultant in software documentation and is co-author of a technical writing textbook, *Readings for Technical Writers.* Dr. Kling was formerly employed as a technical writer for SCS Engineers.

Dr. Kling received her Bachelor's degree from the University of California, Santa Cruz, and completed her M.A. and Ph.D. at the State University of New York at Buffalo. She is a member of the Society for Technical Communication.

ACKNOWLEDGMENTS

Among the many individuals and organizations that have helped in the preparation of this book, I would like to thank the following: Trudy Bergen; Cindy Brown; the Burroughs Corporation; Dr. Bart Childs, Dr. James Kalan, and Dr. Steven Morgan, Department of Computing Science, Texas A&M University; Dr. H.B. Michaelson, Brian E. Ditzler, and the IBM Corporation; Scott Edwards; Dr. Michael Elliott, Executive Director, IEEE Computer Society; Rob Gittins; Janice Ketcham; Dr. Michael Ketcham; Blake Lewis and Source EDP; Scott Marsico; Sue Metzler and Texas Instruments, Inc.; Lucille M. Migatz and the Moore School of Electrical Engineering, University of Pennsylvania; NCR Corporation; Robert Strader; and Bob Winn. The many professional organizations that provided information also deserve recognition, in particular, the Association for Computing Machinery and the IEEE Computer Society for curricula and other information. Thanks, too, to my students whose resumes have been adapted for this book. Finally, I am grateful to my editor, Barbara Wood Donner, for her able assistance on this project, and to Will Kling for reading parts of this book in manuscript and for his many helpful suggestions.

CONTENTS

DEDICATION

To the men and women beginning
their careers in the field.

The Texas Instruments Natural Language Data Base Query System provides a simple menu series readily understandable to nontechnical users. Photo: Texas Instruments Data Systems Group.

CHAPTER 1

INTRODUCTION

The purpose of this book is to inform you about the career opportunities available in computer science: the design, manufacture, and distribution of computers and computing equipment, applications of computers to solve theoretical and practical problems, and the basic theoretical issues of the field.

If you are reading this book, you may already have had some experience with computers. Perhaps you or your family owns a personal computer. Or perhaps you have taken computer programming classes in school or from a computer store. Maybe you are attracted to computer science because you have heard that many well-paid jobs are available.

In this book, you will read about the kinds of work done by computer science professionals in scientific, technical, and engineering environments. You will see how individuals with degrees in computer-related subjects work in data processing and other business applications. You will learn how an interest in marketing and sales can be used to serve the computer needs of industry and the private consumer, and explore some of the special opportunities in documentaion, education, medicine, and other areas.

In this book, we will only consider professional level positions in the computer field: in other words, those career opportunities that usually require a degree from a recognized four-year college or university. There are many opportunities for employment in computer-related positions that do not require a college education. There is a continuous demand for data entry clerks, computer operators, parts fabricators, and computer maintenance personnel. These positions require limited or specialized vocational training only. Some will require no previous training, as all instruction will be provided on the job by the employer. Individuals in these positions contribute significantly to the computer industry. However, discussion of these kinds of employment lies outside the scope of our present interests.

We will also examine the personal characteristics and educational background you will need if you choose to become a computer specialist. You will find advice on selecting a college or university program which will best prepare you for a computer career. We will see how to go about finding your first job, and will describe the employment outlook and directions for future growth of the computer industry.

Reading this book should help you to decide if a career in computer science is for you. It will give you the information you will need if you decide to enter this exciting and rapidly expanding field.

Some Definitions

Computer science is a difficult and demanding subject with its own highly-specialized vocabulary. It will help us, before we begin, to review a few basic terms. In discussing computers, we talk about *hardware,* the physical equipment of a system, and *software,* the sets of instructions (or *programs)* that control the system and tell it how to solve specific problems. Programs are of two types: *applications programs* and *systems programs.* Applications programs are those sets of instructions written to perform a certain task or compute the answer to a particular problem. Systems programs direct, maintain, or otherwise assist the computer to operate and to execute applications programs.

Most of the problem-solving programs are written in *high-level languages* such as FORTRAN, COBOL, Pascal, or PL/1. High-level languages resemble "natural languages" like English. (In fact, most high-level programming languages are English-based, and English is the dominant language of the world-wide computer community.) They are designed to make it easier for people to communicate with the machines. BASIC is a simple high-level language used on most microcomputers.

A computer, however, only understands *machine language*. This means that certain special kinds of systems programs, called *compilers,* must convert high-level languages into a code that will finally be reduced to a series of electronic signals. Other kinds of systems programs, called *operating systems,* oversee and direct all the operations of the machine.

The first step in solving any problem with a computer is to analyze it and develop a logical method for finding the solution. This method is called an *algorithm*. Next, the algorithm will be coded: that is, the programmer will write a program using an appropriate high-level language that gives the computer step-by-step instructions on how to calculate or solve the problem, together with the data needed for its solution. This program will be compiled by the system into *object code* before it can be run, or *executed*. If the program has been successfully written, the *output* will be the answer to the problem. Programs rarely run successfully the first time they are executed, however. Usually, the programmer must go back and find any and all mistakes in the program. This painstaking process is called *debugging*.

In order to solve most real-world problems a program will need to obtain additional information stored in computer *memory*. For instance, a program written to determine the class average on an exam needs to know each student's score. Such information is known as *data*. In *interactive environments,* some of this information can be entered by the programmer or operator from a terminal during program execution. Other information, and all information in *batch environments* or where there is a great deal of stored data, will be retrieved from memory where it has been collected and stored in *files* at some time previous to program execution. Large organized collections (or *libraries)* of information are called *data bases*. Data bases may store information on a company's credit card customers, on all aspects of patient care and billing in a hospital, or on practically any subject. The so-called information revolution, the vast accumulation of knowledge made possible by microelectronics, has made the data base an important means of organizing this flood of facts so that it can be easily accessed and used.

ENIAC, the first electronic computer, was used by the military in the 1940s to calculate ballistics. Photo: The Moore School of Electrical Engineering of the University of Pennsylvania.

CHAPTER 2

A LOOK AT COMPUTERS AND COMPUTER SCIENCE CAREERS

Computers have invaded nearly every area of modern life. In any career you choose, there is a good chance that you will be involved with computers. At the end of 1981, *U.S. News and World Report* estimated that two-thirds of the American work force were involved with collecting, storing, and using information, and this figure continues to grow. The tool which makes this information processing possible is the computer.

The growth in the sheer number of computer systems in the U.S. has been phenomenal (Table I). In 1955, 244 computer systems were in use; by 1980, this number had increased to over 600,000. And as the number of systems has increased, so has the number of computer workers. U.S. Bureau of Labor Statistics figures show that between 1970 and 1978, the percent rate of growth in the employment of computer workers outstripped the overall rate of employment growth in every industry category (see figure on page 9). In the ten years between 1970 and 1980, the number of computer workers more than doubled (Table II).

Computers are used in every industry from agriculture to aerospace. Farmers use computers to time the planting and harvesting of their crops. Ranchers no longer drive their herds to auction; they can sell their livestock in an electronic marketplace made possible by computer networks. In manufacturing, robots are programmed to assemble automobiles, weapons, and the electronic components used in computers themselves: Inventories are maintained, goods stored, and items pulled for sale in computerized warehouses designed to operate without human workers. Computers help send manned spacecraft safely into orbit and aid physicians to diagnose their patients' illnesses.

TABLE I.
GROWTH IN NUMBER OF COMPUTER SYSTEMS IN THE U.S.

Date	Estimated Number of Computer Systems
1955	244
1958	2,550
1964	18,200
1965	26,000
1970	100,000
1980	600,000

Every time you make a plane reservation, phone a friend, or check your bank account statements, you are relying on computers. Computer technology wakes us in the morning, helps us in the kitchen, and follows us when we get into our car to drive to work. Computers can even be programmed to write poetry and to compose music.

TABLE II.
EMPLOYMENT IN COMPUTER OCCUPATIONS, 1970-1980.*

Year	Total	Systems analysts	Programmers	Computer and peripheral equipment operators	Keypunch operators	Computer service technicians
1970	676,037	93,200	161,337	117,222	272,570	31,708
1971	709,000	75,000	158,000	156,000	290,000	30,000
1972	798,000	88,000	186,000	196,000	283,000	45,000
1973	803,000	100,000	187,000	216,000	253,000	47,000
1974	857,000	113,000	199,000	246,000	249,000	50,000
1975	965,000	140,000	223,000	295,000	250,000	57,000
1976	1,000,000	158,000	229,000	287,000	276,000	50,000
1977	1,003,000	150,000	221,000	302,000	280,000	50,000
1978	1,158,000	182,000	247,000	393,000	273,000	63,000
1979	1,352,000	213,000	321,000	453,000	274,000	91,000
1980	1,455,000	243,000	341,000	522,000	266,000	83,000

*Source: *Employment Trends in Computer Occupations.* Washington, DC: U.S. Department of Labor, Bureau of Labor Statistics, 1981.

You can combine an interest in computers with almost any profession or career. In this book, we explore the career opportunities

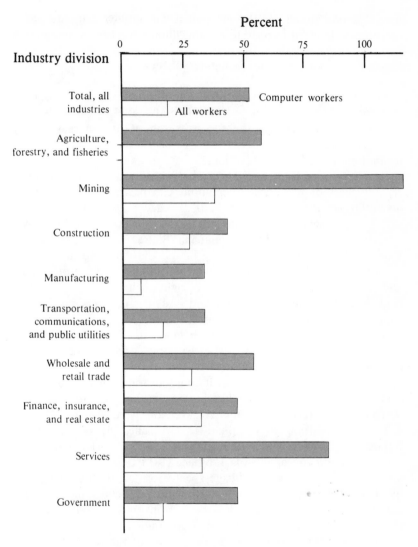

**Percent Change in Employment of Computer Workers
and All Workers by Industry Division, 1970-78**

Source: *Employment Trends in Computer Occupations.* Washington, DC: U.S. Department of Labor, Bureau of Labor Statistics, 1981.

available to individuals who specialize in computer science itself, and want to be at the heart of this challenging new field.

Some Computer History

Modern computers can perform rapid numerical calculations, store and retrieve data of every sort, and make logical decisions that sometimes approach the sophistication of human reasoning. These advanced electronic devices are the result of a number of technological needs and innovations.

People's desire for a mechanism that would reduce the time and repetitiveness of numerical calculations can be traced back to the invention of the abacus over 5,000 years ago. The first real calculating machine in the modern sense, however, was built by French philosopher and mathematician Blaise Pascal (1623-1662). Pascal designed his system of wheels and dials to help his father maintain his business accounts. This first desk-top calculator could add and subtract numbers of up to eight digits. Today, Pascal's contribution to computer science and design is remembered in the computer language that bears his name, Pascal.

In 1642, another philosopher-mathematician, the German Gottfried Wilhelm Leibniz (1646-1716), developed a design for a more complex machine. Leibniz' "Stepped Reckoner" could not only add and subtract like Pascal's device; it could also multiply, divide, and find square roots. An unreliable working version of this machine was built by 1796. By 1820, commercial versions were being sold.

The first real digital computer was designed by an eccentric Englishman named Charles Babbage (1791-1871). Working with his companion and colleague, Ada Lovelace (1815-1852), for whom the language Ada is named, Babbage spent most of his life trying to build his "Analytical Engine." Although a practical model was never completed, Babbage's ideas have been fundamentally important to the theory and design of modern computers.

The next major development in the history of the computer took place in the United States in the last decades of the nineteenth century. Rapid population growth, the result of an increasing tide of European immigration, made it impossible for U.S. census officials to deal with a flood of new statistics. It took officials eight years to finish counting the results of the 1880 census. In order to speed up tabulation of the 1890 census, a young Army engineer and statistician, Hermann Hollerith (1860-1929), constructed an electromechanical device that processed information stored on punched cards. Hollerith's invention reduced by two-thirds the time required to tabulate the census data.

In using punched cards to store information, Hollerith had borrowed an idea from textile technology. The Jacquard loom, invented by Frenchman Joseph Marie Jacquard (1752-1834), used holes punched in cards as patterns to automate the weaving of complicated textile designs. Hollerith used the position of these holes to represent information on an individual's age, sex, nationality, and other vital statistics. Until fairly recently, Hollerith's code was used for computer input (and sometimes output). The code can represent all 26 letters of the alphabet, as well as the digits zero through nine, as an arrangement of holes and spaces. Although punched cards have become obsolete, remnants of Hollerith's code are still used to tell the computer how to read input and format output. And today we know the company originally formed by Hollerith, the Computing Tabulating Recording Company, as IBM.

ENIAC: The first electronic computer. Hollerith's machine was in part electrical, in part mechanical. The first fully electronic calculating machine, ENIAC (the Electronic Numerical Integrator and Computer), was developed in the early 1940's by J. Presper Eckert and John W. Mauchly. ENIAC was designed to help scientists and military personnel calculate the complex equations required by ballistics. It was a bulky construction of vacuum tubes, wiring, and other components. Weighing 30 tons, it took up a 30 by 50 foot room at the University of Pennsylvania's Moore School of Electrical Engineering, where Eckert and Mauchly worked. When fully operational in 1946, ENIAC could perform nearly 5,000 additions or subtractions a second; it could solve in two hours problems in nuclear physics that would have taken one-hundred human engineers an entire year to complete.

ENIAC greatly accelerated the speed of solving complex mathematical problems. However, it could not be programmed in the sense we understand the word today. Rather, it had to be rewired by hand for each new problem. Moreover, whenever one of its nearly 19,000 vacuum tubes failed—which was not infrequently—the system stopped functioning correctly. The invention of the transistor in 1948 at Bell Telephone Laboratories greatly increased the reliability and speed of subsequent computers. It also reduced the machine to a more manageable size. Transistors could be wired onto circuit boards to create permament circuits to hold, send, or convert electrical impulses. These circuits made it possible to "hardwire" basic operations into the computer system itself, and replaced the bulky and fickle vacuum tubes.

John von Neumann. The idea that computer instructions could be stored in the machine itself had been advanced by mathematician John von Neumann (1903-1957) in 1947. His "stored program" notion revolutionized the speed and ease with which the computer could be used to solve problems. With ENIAC, computer instructions were entered into the machine by disconnecting and reconnecting by hand many individual electrical connections. Von Neumann realized that these instructions could be coded as numbers and stored electronically in the same way as numbers used in calculations. This allowed sequences of instructions—programs—to be loaded electronically into the machine, eliminating the time- consuming task of hand setting the instructions sequence for each task.

Von Neumann was also responsible for delimiting the basic structure (or *architecture*) of the modern electronic digital computer: its division into input/output, arithmetic-logic and control units, and memory.

Input and *output* devices enable us to communicate with the computer, giving it raw data and the instructions (or program) to process that information. Output devices supply us with the results of the computer's calculations or data processing operations. As we have seen, in the early days of computing, punched cards were used for both input and output. Today, a variety of different input and output devices are available. Most familiar is the terminal (or alphanumeric keyboard) and television screen, or cathode ray tube (CRT). Combined, these devices are called VDT's (for "video display terminal"). Other input/output devices include optical character readers (OCR's), disks, drums, magnetic tape, and—for output only—a wide variety of printers, some using laser technology to print an astonishing 120 pages per minute.

The *central processing unit* (CPU) is the heart (or, if you will, the brain) of the system. It consists essentially of two parts: an *arithmetic-logic unit* (ALU) and a *control unit*. The control unit monitors all system operations, reading instructions and passing instructions and data to the ALU, where actual computations take place. But the CPU has a limited amount of space or *memory* in which to store data and instructions. Thus additional memory is located outside of the computer core. With the help of the operating system and the executing program, information is fetched from memory and brought into the CPU. The results of each computation are likewise stored in memory.

Most computers currently in use today, from small home computers to large-scale mainframes, conform to this basic structure. New machines, however, are being developed along very different patterns of organization. These machines vastly extend the limits of computational power of the classic von Neumann machine.

Integrated circuits. In the 1950's, advances in memory technology increased the amount of information that could be stored and processed by the computer. Magnetic core, tape, and later (in the 1960's) disk storage dramatically expanded the power of the machines. Improved reliability and increased memory capacity made computers attractive to businesses with large data processing needs. Computers began to appear in business and industry as scientists discovered they could program the machines to select and process alphabetical information as well as operate on numbers.

Computers probably would have remained relatively specialized machines, expensive and with limited applications, without the invention of the semiconductor integrated circuit. Before integrated circuitry, the individual components of the circuitry of a computer or any other electronic device—transistors, capacitors, and so on—were connected by copper wiring. Now, the speed of a computer is a factor of the distance electrical signals must travel. To increase computational speed, this distance must be reduced. Hand-wired circuits and individual components could only be scaled down so far.

By the 1950's, a process called photolithography had been developed that made it possible to "print" the wiring connecting circuit components in much the same way that a photograph is produced from a negative. This made it possible to reduce the distance between components, but, though vastly smaller than the vacuum tubes they had replaced, the components themselves remained relatively large. Researchers came up with a novel idea: if the wiring could be photolithographically printed, would it not be possible to "print" the components themselves using the same process to etch them out of a semiconductive material like silicon? In this way, the wiring and the components of a circuit could be simultaneously produced out of the same layered wafer of semiconductive and other materials. The complexity of the circuit to be produced would determine the number of "printings" necessary. Thus was born the integrated circuit, the field of microelectronics, and the Age of Information of which we are a part.

Although not all computer scientists will agree on exact definitions, they usually speak of the development of the modern computer in terms of "generations" of machines. The first three generations are defined according to the hardware used to process information. First generation machines were made of vacuum tubes and wires; the second generation used transistors, and third generation machines, integrated circuits. Most people think of fourth generation machines as present state-of-the-art computers using Very Large Scale Integration (VSLI): very tiny, very densely packed integrated circuits able to quickly process large amounts of information. "Fifth generation" machines are on the horizon. These machines will fuse hardware and software capabilities in ways that will imitate human thought. Already, machines can be built that out-think humans in special situations: for instance, in playing simple games.

Today, the computational power of ENIAC can be contained on a single microchip. "Supercomputers," extremely powerful number-crunchers like those manufactured by Cray and the Control Data Corporation, can perform over 80 million operations per second.

New developments in computer science theory and applications are occurring daily as the physical and logical limits of present systems are surpassed. The field of computer science offers an unparalleled and exciting opportunity for highly motivated individuals with the right interests, abilities, and education.

Where Do Computer Professionals Work?

Industry sectors. Computer personnel, including programmers, systems analysts, data entry workers, operators, and technicians, work in nearly every sector of the U.S. economy. However, the U.S. Department of Labor estimated in 1978 that eighty percent, or eight out of every ten computer workers, were employed in one of four major industries:

- *Services:* Colleges and universities, accounting and other business services, hospitals and health care facilities all employ computer specialists, primarily in data processing. Computer programming services, which sell programs and computer time to other businesses, employ technical and business computer experts.
- *Manufacturing:* Naturally, the manufacture of computers and peripheral equipment accounts for much of the employment of computer specialists. And as the manufacturing of every kind of product becomes increasingly automated, many computer professionals will be needed to program the production machinery and maintain the automated manufacturing systems.
- *Finance, insurance, real estate:* Banks and insurance companies process vast quantities of data. These industries are principal employers of data processing and information management specialists.
- *Wholesale and retail trade:* Computers are used to control inventory, record sales, and control the daily operations in wholesale and retail business, from the neighborhood supermarket and local department store to industrial suppliers and distributors. Although most people working with computers

in trade are not experts, there are exceptions. First, computer specialists are needed to write programs and develop systems for this industry. Second, many computer specialists are needed to sell computer equipment and software.

Computer personnel are also employed in transportation; communications; public utilities; federal, state, and local government; and the military. Computers and computer professionals are even found in mining, fishing, and agriculture. Computers help tuna fishers off the Pacific coast to find schools of fish, ranchers improve cattle-breeding programs, and farmers predict insect activity that threatens their crops.

It is important to note that the growth of computer use in any industry has so far not been tied to the expansion of that industry. Rather, increased opportunities for computer-related employment are the product of expanded applications of computers to that field.

The computer field is young, dynamic, and rapidly changing. This makes it hard to draw clear distinctions and means that many people with different job titles may perform similar duties. For instance, a field engineer at one company may be called a customer engineer at another. It means, on the other hand, that the same job title may be used to describe different kinds of functions. A programmer/analyst in a bank may have very different responsibilities than someone with the same title working for an engineering firm. In general, though, we can divide computer professionals into two main classes: computer science and engineering specialists, and information and data processing specialists.

Computer specialists are mainly interested in computer hardware, software, and computing theory. These individuals work to design and develop new equipment, systems and applications software, and computer systems. They enjoy the technical problems of computers and computing, are more technically oriented, and may prefer working with machines and systems to working with people.

Information specialists, sometimes called EDP (for "Electronic Data Processing") specialists, are more interested in computer applications. They are especially interested in using computer systems as effectively as possible to process and evaluate information. They tend to be more business than engineering oriented, and often seek out opportunities to work with people with little or no computing expertise.

At present, many college programs in computer science allow students to specialize either in technical and engineering topics or in business applications and information management. However, as both the computer industry matures and education of computer professionals becomes more standarized, we will see an ever-greater distinction between computer scientists and information/data processing specialists. This distinction already operates to a large extent today within the computer industry and in industries employing computer personnel.

Employers. In the jargon of computer professionals, employers are divided into two groups: *vendors* of computer equipment, systems, software, or services; and *end-users* (or just "users"), organizations and individuals that use computer systems to help them in their work.

The computer industry is currently the fourth largest industry in the world. Naturally, then, many computer professionals find employment within this industry working for vendors. Vendors include manufacturers of large and small general purpose computing systems. Many of these vendors have become almost household words: IBM, Apple, Texas Instruments, Hewlett Packard. Other vendors specialize in special purpose computers or peripheral equipment: stand-alone word processors, telecommunications systems, terminals, printers, plotters, optical character readers, and so on. Yet another class of vendor sells software, or packaged programs, to perform any of a nearly infinite range of special applications: manage a business, control a production process, or play a game, to name a few. These "software houses" hire programmers to create these special packages. Finally, computer service companies sell various computing services to those businesses which do not have their own in-house facilities. They may also provide maintenance and consulting services to end-user organizations.

End-users also employ computer professionals. In large user organizations in such fields as aerospace, avionics, defense, and other engineering-oriented areas, there may be up to four classes of employees whose work involves computers:

- *Systems specialists.* Systems specialists maintain the hardware and software for the community of computer users within the organization. They usually hold degrees in computer science.
- *Special applications experts.* These individuals, who often hold graduate degrees in computer-related subjects, are responsible for developing very specialized applications for computers related to the main work or products of the organization. For instance, they may design a computer system to perform on-board processing of information in a weather satellite or to guide a missile to its target.
- *Computer users.* These individuals are involved in original research, analysis, or development. They may be analyzing geophysical data to locate oil reserves or developing new telecommunications technologies: that is, they are involved in the main work of their employing organization. For the most part, these individuals are mathematicians, physicists, or other scientific or engineering experts. While they may know a great deal about computing, they remain essentially sophisticated users of computers, not computer specialists.
- *Information systems and data processing personnel.* Any large organization requires information and data processing specialists to manage and maintain the day-to-day flow of data, including payroll, scheduling, and other routine tasks as well as large-scale management of computing resources and information accessibility.

Most user organizations hire information specialists. Banks, insurance companies, and other financial institutions are major employers of information and data processing specialists. Data processing experts also find opportunities in any large corporation or business where there is a need for financial reports, analysis of business trends, or where records need to be maintained.

Is Computer Science for You?

Certainly, the computer field presents many rewarding career opportunities. However, is it the right field for you? You should go through three steps in making a career decision:

- Identify your skills, aptitudes, and interests.
- Identify a career or profession where you can use your skills.
- Identify the education and practical job experience you will need to attain your career goals in your chosen occupation.

In order to identify your aptitudes and interests, begin by asking yourself some simple questions. What classes have you done well in, and enjoyed, in school? What are your hobbies and extracurricular activities? How do you like to spend your free time? Make a list of what you feel to be your major accomplishments: Which have been most important to you? Which have given you greatest satisfaction?

Your school counseling or placement office may be able to help you assess your abilities. Standardized vocational guidance testing is often available. Your school may even have a computerized vocational guidance program, like the Educational Testing Service's SIGI.

Many books available in your library or local bookstore are good sources of vocational advice. One book that you may find very helpful in identifying your particular talents is Richard Bolles' widely read *What Color Is Your Parachute?* Published by the Tandem Press, Bolles' book is updated annually and includes a good deal of practical career advice.

What kind of person will do well in computer science? How do you know if computing is for you? For some people, an aptitude for computer science may be as obvious as a gift for music or mathematics. If you are a computer whiz or natural programmer, someone with endless curiosity about and enthusiasm for the machines and what they do, you have probably already decided to go into computer science and are reading this book to find out how to do it.

But what if you are not yet certain that computer science is for you? If you have not yet decided on a career, you must ask yourself to what extent you have the attributes of a successful computer expert. Computers are logical, and they reward logical thought. If you are logical, systematic, and patient, if you enjoy solving problems or puzzles, computing may be for you. Mathematical abilities are important in systems programming, scientific and engineering applications, and in research and development. Math is less important in business and data processing applications, although you can still expect to work with numbers. And written and oral communication skills are very important.

The following list summarizes the traits of the type of individual who is likely to find computer science a rewarding and satisfying profession:

- A capacity for logical thought
- Analytical skills: enjoys solving problems or puzzles
- Mental ingenuity or cunning: an ability to see more than one way to do something
- Interested in mathematics
- Painstaking attention to detail
- Persistence: able to stick with a problem until it is completely worked out
- Good communication skills

In addition to these traits, you must have well-developed study habits if you are to prepare for a career in computer science. You must also enjoy and be committed to learning. A degree in computer science is only the first step in your education as a professional in this field. The pace of development and the variety of individual applications mean that the computer scientist's education never stops. On-the-job and continuing education is a given.

If you possess these attributes together with a mechanical aptitude and like the idea of working with computer hardware, the electrical "nuts and bolts" of the machines, you may wish to consider the related field of electrical engineering. If you are intrigued by the connection between machine and program, are attracted by the problem-solving challenge of programming, want to learn about the theoretical problems behind a computer system and its organization, or are interested in the ways computers can be used in other fields, computer science may be for you.

The range of opportunities for individuals with computer science expertise is vast. You could share in the design and programming of ever-faster, more powerful machines. As a member of a project team, you might program and track the flight of the space shuttle, or develop special systems that enable blind persons to "see," the deaf to "hear" again. You might study the way we think and speak, in order to create an intelligent computer that imitates human thought or understands human speech. You might gain satisfaction from teaching others how to use and enjoy computers. You might work in business applications in banking or insurance. You could manage the information system of a hospital or university, or help businesses to select, install, and maintain a computer system that meets their specific needs. These and many other possiblities are yours if you choose to pursue a career in computer science.

Careful testing of equipment is important at all stages of manufacturing.
Photo: upper, NTC stock; lower, Texas Instruments Data Systems Group.

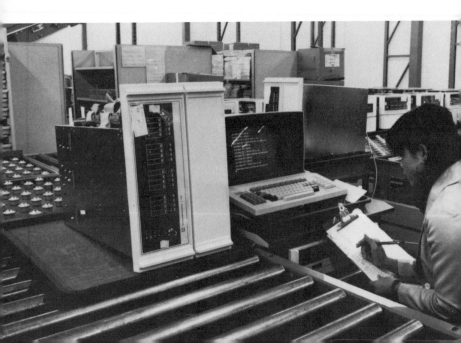

CHAPTER 3

OPPORTUNITIES WITH A TECHNICAL OR ENGINEERING EMPHASIS

In this chapter, we will examine the kinds of positions available in technical and engineering environments or which emphasize technical and scientific programming skills. This will include:

- *Hardware/software.* Hardware positions are predominantly found with computer vendors. Positions in systems (software) programming are available with vendors, software houses and computer service firms, and in some user organizations. Most scientific and engineering applications programmers work for users.

- *Operations.* Operations encompasses the day-to-day operation of a computer facility, most often within user organizations of every sort: government agencies, universities, hospitals, businesses, or anywhere a medium to large, complex, multi-purpose computer system is found. Vendors also have their own in-house computer operations staff.

- *Research and development of hardware and software.* Many hardware and some software positions are in research and development. Most R&D positions are found with vendors and in large user organizations that develop special-purpose or "embedded" computer products. An embedded product is a computer system which is a part or component of a larger product: for instance, a microprocessor that regulates auto exhaust emissions.

Because the computer and related industries are growing and changing so rapidly, it is impossible for us to cover every opportunity that exists in the technical and engineering environment. Rather, we will look at some typical career opportunities and profiles to give you an idea of what it would be like to work in this area.

HARDWARE

The word *hardware* is used to designate the physical units or equipment that make up a computer system: the computer itself and its network of circuitry, as well as peripheral equipment such as terminals, printers, and tape drives.

Computer scientists and computer engineers aid electrical engineers and other equipment design specialists to design, develop, and test computer hardware and peripheral equipment. Design of hardware can range from the creation of a single computer chip, such as IBM's 512K chip, to an entire computer system or product. But since more powerful computers are made up of an array of microprocessors and memory chips, much of the work in hardware takes place at the chip level.

Peripheral equipment may be developed in conjunction with CPU design as part of a total system. Or it may be developed independently. Some companies, like Qume, a maker of printers, specialize in producing peripherals that can be used with CPU's built by many different manufacturers. Increasingly, microprocessors are being built into terminals. These "smart" terminals are in essence small computers. Desk-top work stations, stand-alone word processors, and similar office automation products combine chip and peripheral design into one package.

A hardware product begins as an idea or concept. A team of engineers and computer science experts will get together and ask: "What would we (or the market) like to see in a product? What would we like it to do?" Once the general idea is sketched out, a set of engineering specifications is developed. These specifications express in complete detail the performance, design, and materials' (if appropriate) characteristics of the product. The next step is to build a prototype, or working model, which is tested, debugged, and perfected before full-scale manufacturing begins.

What does this process involve at the chip level? Once the performance specifications have been formalized, electrical and computer engineers develop logic and circuit designs. These patterns lay out the path electrons will travel as signals are pulsed through the chip. These circuit designs are photographically enlarged and studied. Any flaws are corrected. Then, each circuit design is reduced to a "photomask" or negative which is used to etch or imprint the circuit onto a silicon wafer. The manufacture of silicon chips is complex and must take place under extremely sterile conditions. One bit of dust can make a chip unusable. The technology that has been developed to manufacture computer chips is extraordinarily sophisticated; many manufacturing procedures are closely guarded secrets.

Before chips go into full production, the prototype is rigorously tested to locate any potential error. Computer scientists specializing in testing write special programs to evaluate prototype performance. At every stage in the development of computer hardware and at any level, testing and evaluation is crucial. To detect the slightest potential for error, test specialists try to subject the prototype to all possible input situations. Many flaws are only found through endless trial and error testing.

As a specialist in hardware, you may be involved in logic design and testing, microprogramming, systems design—linking individual chips into a fully-operational computer system—and systems evaluation. All work in hardware requires a solid background in electrical engineering. You should plan your undergraduate program to include hardware, electrical engineering, and physics courses if you wish to work in this area. You should consider college curricula that specialize in computer engineering.

SOFTWARE

In the early days of computers and computing, emphasis was on improving hardware design to increase the speed and reliability of operations. When integrated circuitry was introduced in the 1960's, though, machines became virtually fail-safe and much less costly. From this point on, many, if not most computer errors could really be attributed to human error: that is, to errors in software programming. Moreover, the extension of computer applications into many areas of life depends on writing new sets of instructions to tell the machine how to perform new tasks. Today, many industry experts feel the astonishingly rapid advances in hardware technology are over. They believe that, while hardware development will continue, the most exciting and creative advances in the future will take place in software.

Software Engineering

As hardware costs have declined and the complexity and range of computer applications has increased, the problems of creating these large, extraordinarily detailed programs (or *software systems*) have become critical. *Software engineering* provides an efficient and coherent method of approaching the design, development, and maintenance of such large software systems. And *software engineer* is a job category gaining in importance and status.

Software is expensive to create because it is labor-intensive. That is, it takes many people working for a long time to write a complex program. Industry estimates suggest that an average programmer can write only eight to ten lines of debugged code a day. Software engineering recognizes the high cost of software and uses various techniques to control these costs. It also recognizes that the kinds of real-world problems most software systems are designed to handle change in time. Software engineering builds in ways to modify these programs to account for such changes. And by approaching the design and maintenance of large programs in a systematic fashion, software engineering ideally results in a more reliable product.

Central to software engineering is the idea of the *software life-*

cycle, which breaks the design, development, and maintenance of large programs into a series of interrelated steps:

- Identification of *what* the software must be able to do. This is sometimes called "requirements engineering" and produces the "requirements specification."
- Description of *how* the software will accomplish the tasks it must do. In this stage, software engineers develop a "design specification" that outlines major sections of the program.
- Implementation. At this point, members of a programming team work individually to code and debug segments of the program. *Structured programming* techniques, first proposed by E. Dijkstra in 1968, enable the software engineer to see the program as a series of separate units. Each unit can be assigned to a different programmer, then assembled into the overall software system.
- Testing and validation. In this phase, the program is tested using sample input to make sure that it performs correctly and to locate any possible sources of errors.
- Operations and maintenance. The task of the software engineer is not over when the system is installed and running. Maintaining and updating the program continue as long as it is being used. It is estimated that between 40 to 60 percent of the money spent on software goes to its maintenance.

To go into software engineering, you need at minimum an undergraduate degree in computer science and course-work in software engineering and structured programming techniques. A master's degree that emphasizes software engineering or considerable experience as a member of a programming team in a software engineering situation are alternate means of entry into this area.

The Programming Team

Programmers almost always work as part of a project team. This team usually includes a project leader or manager, who may be a software engineer or a senior systems analyst. The project leader is responsible for overall program design and assigns programming tasks to other team members. This individual is assisted by an experienced senior programmer who supervises other programmers, checks their work, and confers with the project leader when problems arise. Programmers translate the design specifications into computer code. They work on small segments of the program at a time, writing code, using sample data to test and debug each piece of code, making changes to eliminate errors in their segments.

Most project teams also include support personnel who are not computer scientists but who provide valuable assistance. An administrator will handle the allocation of money, office space, personnel, and equipment. This frees the project leader to attend to technical problems. A technical writer will work with programmers to document the program as it is written. Secretarial staff will be there to handle daily office routine, and a program librarian may be assigned to keep track of the status of program segments. Of course, the size and composition of the project team varies with the scope and complexity of the project.

Most recent computer science graduates will begin as junior programmers or coders, working on a project that may already be well-advanced. Beginning programmers work to modify sections of code written by more senior programmers, then progress to write sections of original code and to develop testing procedures for debugging.

Working as part of a project team can be an intense experience. Most projects are completed under extreme time pressure: it may not matter how elegantly you write a program. The point is to get it done, to get the system up and running. Most programming teams work against deadlines set by other divisions of their organization. It is not uncommon for team members to work afterhours and even on weekends when a deadline is approaching. Nor is hardware design a less intense environment. The same pressures and conditions exist.

To work successfully under such stressful conditions requires more than merely technical competence. Nerves are frayed, tempers are short, people are anxious and often very tired. Patience, self-control, sensitivity to the feelings and concerns of other team

members, and simple stamina are valuable traits in such cir-
cumstances. These traits may have little to do with a programmer's
technical ability.

Systems Software Programming

Systems programmers specify, design, and develop operating
systems, compilers, assemblers, utility and data base management
programs, and other kinds of software that direct entire computer
systems and enable applications programs to be processed. Systems
programmers also install, debug, and maintain systems software
once it is in place.

Systems programmers may work for computer and peripheral
manufacturers, computer service companies, management consulting firms, or in user organizations. Working for computer
manufacturers, systems programmers work with design teams to
develop new computer systems or products and to upgrade existing
systems. They often assist in the installation of a system purchased
by a user and may train the user's personnel in the use of their new
system.

Working in a user environment, systems software programmers
support their organization's computer operations and applications
programming. They help applications people to evaluate their computing needs, and insure that all systems function efficiently and
without error. They modify vendor software packages to meet the
needs of their own company and in some cases are responsible for
the security of the computer system.

The proliferation of mini- and microcomputers in a variety of industries and applications has created a need for systems programmers who can work with distributed systems. The systems programming requirements for a network of small computers differ from
those of a centralized mainframe computer. Systems programmers
with expertise in data communications, networking, data base concepts, and terminal systems are very much in demand at present.

Systems programmers may work mainly with assembly languages
rather than with the high-level languages used in applications programming. These languages are closer to the code of ones and zeros

that the machine understands than they are to the more "natural" high-level languages. Assembly language programming is rigorous and extremely detailed. It demands of the programmer not only acute analytical skills, but patience, persistence, and precision. It also takes a special sort of intuitive problem-solving creativity that most systems programmers will talk about but find difficult to define. People who go into systems programming tend to be more interested in problems in pure computer science than in the kinds of problems in science, technology, and business that are of principal concern to applications programmers. Systems programmers also need some interest in hardware.

Systems software programmers usually begin, like most programmers, as coders working on programs designed and developed by systems groups. They may advance through senior systems programmer level to work as a systems project leader, heading a team of systems specialists in the design and implementation of systems software. Advancement in user organizations can lead to operations management and technical support positions.

Engineering and/or Scientific Applications Programming

Applications programmers working in a scientific or engineering environment design, code, test, and debug programs to solve specific technical or theoretical problems. These problems almost always involve complex mathematical calculations. Programmers in this field also help to develop the hardware, software, and input/output specifications for computer systems used in scientific and engineering applications.

Engineering and scientific applications programmers work in many different industries, including aerospace and avionics, defense-related research and development, telecommunications, manufacturing, medical research and treatment, the oil and gas industry, and in all fields of engineering. Computer vendors also employ engineering applications programmers to assist in product development and support. Some companies sponsor high-level research related to physics and mathematics. Much programming on these projects will be done by the researchers themselves, assisted by applications programmers.

Applications programmers in a scientific or engineering environment aid in the work that pushes science and technology beyond the limits of the present. They may solve problems in "real-time" control systems, where the computer must sense external conditions and respond immediately: for instance, in the computer system that guides a missile in its flight from launch to target or controls the temperature of a manufacturing process. They may write software to link a network of minicomputers into a single, fully automated production line, or that processes the images beamed back to earth from space. Applications programmers use special simulation or graphics languages to develop models to improve the flow of raw materials through a manufacturing plant or of air around the surface of an accelerating automobile. They write programs to plot the orbit of a satellite, probe the depths of the earth in search of oil, track the path of an approaching hurricane, or predict the long-range effects of a disaster on the surrounding population and environment.

A programmer specializing in scientific and engineering applications will use languages such as FORTRAN, the most widely used language for scientific programming, Pascal, and assembly languages. Newer languages, including C (a high-level language which allows some assembly-type operations) and Ada are becoming more and more important. Ada, a language commissioned by the U.S. Department of Defense to replace FORTRAN, will soon be required for all Defense contract work. Since so many projects in aerospace, energy, and military research are funded by the DOD, Ada is expected to become far more widely used than it is at present.

In addition to a knowledge of assembly and high-level program[7] ming languages, you must have excellent mathematical skills to work in this field. You also need good interpersonal skills and the ability to listen. Scientific and engineering applications programmers work in tightly-knit small teams and must often confer with scientists or engineers to determine what their problems are, what input they can supply, and what output they expect. Because of the high level of mathematical and technical knowledge this kind of programming requires, many people working in the field today hold degrees in mathematics, physics or other sciences, or in an engineering discipline other than computer science.

OPERATIONS

The operations staff works in a computing or data processing center to keep the computer system running. It is hard to make generalizations about computer operations because so much depends on the size of the installation. In a small facility, one college-trained individual may be responsible for every aspect of computer operations. In large computing centers, the staff can be sizable, with a resultant range in job titles and specializations. Personnel can include junior, senior, and lead computer operators, peripheral equipment operators, hardware technicians, job-control clerks, data entry staff, librarians, shift supervisors, and a technical support staff, all overseen by an operations manager.

Operators keep track of computer operations from one or more consoles in the machine room where the CPU and some peripheral equipment is located. Operators coordinate the flow of jobs through the system. They mount and dismount the tapes or disks which store programs, input, and output, and make sure that all equipment is operating smoothly. When something does go wrong, operators attempt to restore normal operations or notify the person in charge of troubleshooting—usually the operations manager. Because operators know their system so well, their description of breakdowns can be essential in returning it to working order.

Data entry (or keypunch) clerks enter data into files that will be processed by the computer. They usually do this by typing data in at terminals located throughout the building rather than in the machine room itself. In the early days of computers, data was keypunched onto cards. Keypunches have virtually disappeared from a modern computing facility, but the term "keypunch" survives.

Hardware technicians service and maintain the terminals, printers, modems, drives, and other equipment. *Job-control clerks* log work orders and jobs as they come into the computer operations center, handle and burst printouts, and deliver output to users, if necessary. In many facilities, these tasks overlap with those performed by operators. In interactive or distributed data processing environments, some of these tasks may disappear.

Most computing and data processing centers have a *librarian* or librarians to catalogue and file magnetic tapes and disks, keep this material in good condition, and check it out as it is needed for specific jobs. *Program librarians* are responsible for cataloguing and maintaining programs. Sometimes program librarians will work as members of a programming team to keep track of sections of code as they are written and record the status of testing, debugging, and completion of each piece of software.

The *technical support staff* maintains systems software and deals with any problems that can be traced to that software. They may also write customized programs for special purposes. In addition, they talk with users to make sure their applications programs can be run effectively.

People working in computer operations have long been considered the manual laborers of the computer world. Jobs were (and often still are) low-paying and offered limited opportunities for advancement. It is still true that most of the routine jobs in computer operations do not require a college degree or specialized training. Today, however, operators, operations managers, and members of the technical support staff are all expected to have a high degree of technical knowledge of and experience in systems programming and job control language (JCL). This generally translates into a college degree in computer science or a computer-related subject.

Computers run 24 hours a day, seven days a week. Operations personnel work in shifts and on weekends. This makes part-time jobs in operations very attractive for students, who can schedule work around their classes. And the practical experience gained working in operations will make your coursework much more understandable and relevant. It is an excellent way to learn about the machines. Also, employers look favorably on computer science graduates with such down-to-earth experience.

Computing or Data Processing Center Operations Management

The manager of a computing or data processing center directs and oversees all aspects of computer operations. His or her main responsibility is to keep the computer, peripheral equipment, and software in good working order. In other words, the operations manager works to keep the system running smoothly, efficiently, and without error.

The operations manager almost always works in intermediate to large organizations, such as hospitals, universities, banks, or large businesses, where a great deal of computing and/or data processing is done. Most operations managers work with mainframe computers in large-scale data base and communications-oriented environments. They are in charge of all aspects of the system and staff, including scheduling of jobs, quality control, and maintenance of systems and some applications software. To do this, they supervise a number of people in the machine room and on the data processing center staff. They also work with users or the managers of user departments to provide the facilities these departments need. For instance, in a university computing center, the operations manager may need to guarantee that the system provides output to the admissions office, the registrar, and the payroll and personnel division. At the same time, the system may be used by professors involved in research that requires computing and by students for instructional purposes. A large system must be many things to many users. The operations manager coordinates these diverse demands on the system and ensures that it functions for all purposes and all users. In smaller installations, the operations manager's responsibilities are much the same, although the size of his or her staff and the range of system applications is more limited.

The operations manager is in part a supervisor. He or she also must be able to communicate with users who may know relatively little about computing. Nonetheless, this job remains essentially technical in nature. The operations manager works with the machine. He or she must have a high level of hardware and operating systems software expertise and a good deal of practical experience with large computer systems. This job also takes a certain amount of psychological resilience, for the operations manager must answer for any problem in the system. In the final analysis, when something goes wrong and the machine goes down, it is the operations manager's problem.

Technical Support Services Management

The technical support staff is responsible for maintaining the operating systems software of an intermediate to large computer center, most often in user organizations. Technical support groups also develop and maintain special-purpose software such as the telecommunications and data base management programs that link remote computers and peripheral equipment to the central system. The manager of the technical support group supervises systems software programmers, schedules work, assists in troubleshooting, and takes part in planning and evaluation of the overall system. If additional hardware or software is being considered, the technical support manager will be involved in the decision. He or she also talks with users having problems running their applications programs on the system and with vendors of systems software packages to find out what might be causing a particular problem and how to fix it.

To become the manager of a technical support group, you need considerable experience in systems programming. Commonly, the manager is promoted from within the support group staff. You must be willing to supervise and account for the work done by your staff and be acutely aware of the technical niceties and limitations of your system and its software. This position is not one for people who are easily frustrated, as discovering the reason for a glitch (or error) often takes all the skill and patience of a master detective, as well as an almost-intuitive understanding of the system. For those problem-oriented, creative systems programmers, though, who want to stay in primarily technical positions, technical support management is a good career goal.

RESEARCH AND DEVELOPMENT

Research is the study of the fundamental physical and theoretical problems in a field, without direct concern for practical applications. Development applies the findings of basic research to solve concrete problems or to design products that fulfill specific needs or perform particular tasks. Of course, the line between basic research and practical applications is never clear. Advances in theoretical knowledge make it possible to develop new products. At the same time, new innovations in technology may shed light on previously unexplained theoretical questions. And in fact, most corporate research in computer science is closely tied to product development and manufacturing support. Much applied research takes place in vendor organizations, while more theoretical research is typically done in university settings, often supported by funding from industry.

The development of a new computer product involves much more than its simple design. It includes following a product from its first idea through its manufacturing and marketing phases. It may include changing or upgrading the product as it is improved or as customers need additional features. Most computer software, for instance, is periodically updated by its vendor. This means all users must be notified and changes in individual installations made. In fact, from a computer vendor's point of view, development does not end until a product is withdrawn from the market.

Positions in research and development are available in nearly every area of computer science, including computational methods and numerical analysis (developing new algorithms and solving difficult problems in advanced mathematics); computer organization and architecture (devising ways to improve computer performance by changing the relation of its parts and structure); systems design and systems science (studying computer operations and applications as a network of functions); programming systems and languages (pushing the applications of computers in new directions through increased knowledge of programming techniques, linguistics, and natural languages); and information science (designing ways to make more information more readily available to users). Many positions in research and development require graduate study; a few require a Ph.D. in computer science or a related discipline.

Current Directions in Research

There has probably never been a time in the brief history of computer science when the opportunities in research were so varied and exciting. It is, of course, impossible to begin to describe all of the many directions in which research is proceeding today. Some of the more visible areas, though, include those associated with fifth-generation computer projects.

Fifth-generation computers represent a radical leap in performance and design from the first four generations of computers. Two kinds of fifth-generation systems are under development: *supercomputers,* large, general-purpose computers that can process millions of instructions a second to perform exceedingly complex calculations in science and engineering; and *intelligent machines,* computers that use information in a rational, human-like manner. These machines depend on advances in a number of areas.

Computer architecture. The first four generations of computers were based on the structure (or "architecture") associated with John von Neumann; all processed a sequential string of instructions and could deal with only one instruction at a time. Improvements in computational speed resulted from increasingly compact, reliable circuitry. In order to make the quantuum leap in performance that the fifth-generation machines require, this one-operation-at-a-time architecture must be surpassed. Researchers believe that parallel processing—linking a number of processors together, each of which simultaneously executes an instruction—will expand the computational limits of present machines. We know that the human brain is able to process many kinds of information at the same time: we can listen to the radio, smoke a cigarette, and drive a car through the rush hour traffic. Presumedly, we think and make decisions on the basis of multiple stimuli. Designing a computer that can compute more quickly or "think" in human terms will depend in part on developments in parallel processing.

Very large-scale integrated circuits. The microelectronics revolution that replaced slide rules with pocket calculators and placed the computer next to the television set in many American homes was made possible by integrated circuitry and the silicon chip. And while most research efforts today focus on advanced software, this software runs on microprocessors and memory chips. The research problems in VSLI include inventing new design techniques to improve the way these miniaturized circuits perform and manufacturing techniques that enable up to one million transistors to be crammed onto a single chip that can be economically mass produced. IBM's 512K chip represents the direction of VSLI research, which covers work in basic physics, circuit design, materials and manufacturing, and developing improved ways to link chips together.

Artificial intelligence. Perhaps the most exciting and most promising research today is in the field of artificial intelligence. What do we mean when we speak of "intelligence"? And how do we build a computer system that fits our definition? Researchers in artificial intelligence use special languages like LISP and PROLOG to develop programs that model human reasoning. Particular applications of artificial intelligence research include natural language processing and voice recognition; image processing and pattern recognition; and expert systems.

Natural language processing and voice recognition. Computer scientists, working with linguists and psychologists, are trying to make it possible for people to speak directly to computers as they do to one another. This means teaching the computer to recognize and process ordinary human speech. If perfected, natural language processing will free the user from having to learn a special computer language like FORTRAN or BASIC. Systems already exist that can respond to a limited vocabulary of voice commands, but the day when we speak to our computer in the same way we speak to our friends or fellow workers is some ways in the future.

Image processing and pattern recognition. Many of the projected applications of advanced computer technology depend on teaching machines to "see": that is, to recognize and identify shapes and objects and respond to that visual input. Advances in robotics and automated manufacturing, for instance, are tied to developments in this area. Again, some rudimentary advances have been made. Digital processing of images is fairly advanced. And researchers in military applications have taught a computer to segment (or isolate) a cartoon image from its background and track it across the screen. Still, much work remains to be done before computers will be able to see and process images in anything that approaches our own ability.

Expert systems and knowledge engineering. Expert systems are software packages that incorporate facts about a subject and a human expert's ways of interpreting those facts. Researchers in expert systems distinguish between *data* (and data processing) and *information* (and information processing). Data are raw facts: your body temperature, heart rate, and rate of respiration are data. Information gives meaning, significance, or value to raw facts. The knowledge that a body temperature of 104°F is dangerously high is information. Expert systems combine this information into a knowledge base and guide the processing of program input according to "rules of thumb" or *heuristics*. These rules of thumb are supplied by human experts and built into the software. *Knowledge engineers* specialize in the construction of these complex and difficult programs. They work closely with scientists, physicians, or other experts. Some observers believe that knowledge engineering will be a powerful force in the future. They argue that many decisions made today by people will eventually be made by expert systems.

One exciting potential of expert systems research is that it provides a way for exceptional human knowledge and experience to be recorded, shared, and passed on to others. The expert system gives to its creators a kind of immortality. Moreover, the knowledge of many experts can be pooled to build a system that surpasses the ability of any single human expert. And that causes some people to worry that expert systems might put an end to our need for human experts.

TWO CAREER PROFILES

Operating Systems Programmer

Although Rob received his B.S. in computer science barely five years ago, he has an impressive fifteen years' experience in computing. He was introduced to computing at fourteen, writing programs in BASIC in his junior-high computer lab. He was not impressed. If BASIC was all there was to computers, he thought, there's nothing special here: anyone can do it. But at sixteen, he learned FORTRAN and then ALGOL, a language similar to IBM assembly that is used on Burroughs machines. This was something else. As he says, he "started fooling around and did things I shouldn't have." But in the process, he learned ALGOL and the Burroughs system well enough to write a small calculator program. At this point he became, as he says, "addicted to computing."

Rob was fortunate enough to attend a large metropolitan high school with a special program in computer science. He spent three to four hours a day on the terminals during his last two years. At eighteen, he got his first full-time job as an operator/programmer at a construction company. He was able to pay for his college education through a series of jobs in programming and operations, working full-time in his senior year in college.

When he graduated from college, Rob accepted a position as a systems programmer for a major computer vendor. He developed special in-house systems management programs for that company's own computing needs, then joined a project design team. Their goal: to develop a smart computer terminal. Rob wrote about 80% of the software for the terminal. He recalls that this, like many design projects, did not flow smoothly from concept to prototype to production. The first circuit board the team came up with proved faulty; the circuitry had to be redesigned. Eventually, though, the terminal was completed; today, it is sold throughout the U.S.. Rob describes the special satisfaction that completing a project of this sort gives: "It's a neat feeling," he says, "when you see something you worked on very hard make it to market and be liked."

Today, Rob is part of the technical staff of a medium-sized telecommunications company. His job title is manager of the operating systems group for desk-top work station products. These are compact devices that combine the features of a telephone, computer, and other functions into a single unit. Rob joined his present employer because he wanted to work on products that would more directly affect the people that use them. As a terminal designer, Rob was working with embedded software, or *firmware*: that is, programs that would be built into the terminal itself and never be seen by users. Today, he works on programs that people see and use directly. This is in accord with his belief that computer science is about helping people make their lives easier.

Rob's daily responsibilities include minimal management duties supervising a small team of operating systems programmers. He is principal systems architect for the operating system design of a new desk-top work station product. In this capacity, he negotiates with hardware designers to determine the hardware features of the system. This, he feels, is probably the most important aspect of his job because it directly affects the actual production of the product.

Rob thinks that computer science is slowly becoming a true science. From his own experience, he will tell you that it is a very worthwhile science to approach. But his emphasis is on the word, *science.* Students considering the field are warned not to limit themselves just to programming. Rather, they should take every opportunity to learn as much as possible about the underlying principles of the field. Additionally, as someone who hires other computer science graduates, Rob advises those interested in research and development to obtain a master's degree in computer science. This, he feels, is rapidly becoming the standard base-level degree for work in R&D, while the B.S. degree typically leads to applications programming positions.

Engineering Programmer, Software Engineering

Scott E. is a technical person who is in the process of directing his career toward management. He works for a vendor of intermediate-sized computer systems as an engineering programmer.

In the evenings, he takes courses at a local university and is working towards his Master's in Business Administration (M.B.A.). His employer encourages and pays for this additional education.

Four years ago, Scott received his B.S. in computer science from a large public university. His minor in engineering technology gave him hands-on training in electronics. This practical experience is useful to him in his present position as a member of a hardware design team.

In Scott's experience, a typical design project has three phases. First, there is a brainstorming period where the team decides what they want to do, what technology is available or needs to be created to get the project done, and where the market will be when their new product is ready to be released. Next, specifications are developed that outline the step-by-step procedure to be followed to convert an idea into a real product. Scott says that at this stage, the team is working out "what goes on in the black box we're creating." This leads to the technical blueprint, or engineering specifications, that the team will work with. During the third and longest phase of a project, Scott says "We roll up our sleeves and start getting the product out—hardware, software, documentation." A short project might last eight months. On average, most teams work together for eighteen months to two years.

Scott is good at what he does. He enjoys what he describes as "a feeling of satisfaction that you can go from point A—the specifications—to point Z—the final implementation—and get the whole thing working properly." Why, then, is he working on an M.B.A.? In part, because he sees only limited possibilities for advancement. He points out that there is only so much need for "technical horsepower." And this need can be met by each year's crop of college graduates who do the real "grunt work"—coding— on a project. A very few people will carve out a special place for themselves as a technical "guru" in any company; for most, the technical path is not, as Scott sees it, extremely realistic. The more likely path to advancement leads to management. And as a realist, Scott knows that an M.B.A. will enable him to move up in his company. Or he can use his technical and business knowledge to start his own consulting business. For the present, the knowledge he gains from his business courses continually improves his daily job performance.

Scott believes firmly in the relation of practical work experience and formal education. He recommends that students in computer science "get experience as soon as possible." Experience, he says, will help you find out what you want to do. It helps you learn "what this nebulous term programming is and how it relates to you" and your interests. He suggests cooperative education programs, summer jobs, or part-time work in computer operations on your college campus as good ways to gain experience.

Most data processing jobs involve working at a computer terminal. Photo: Bell & Howell Education Group.

CHAPTER 4

OPPORTUNITIES IN BUSINESS DATA PROCESSING, MANAGEMENT, AND MARKETING

In scientific and engineering applications, most computer functions involve complicated mathematical calculations. In business applications, the math is much simpler. It's not all that difficult, for example, to add up all credit card purchases a customer has made, subtract the payments, and figure out how much is owed. The problem is the sheer volume of information that must be processed and recorded. Thus, many computer-related jobs in a business environment are jobs in data processing.

Computer specialists will find a multitude of career opportunities in business data processing. In addition, opportunities exist in marketing and sales as well as management. While it is true that most of the "leading-edge" computer work is found in the technical and engineering sector, the greatest demand for employees comes from the business world. It is estimated that business applications and data processing account for about 80 percent of all computer cycling, or run time, in the United States today. Career opportunities are diverse and offer many chances for advancement. In this chapter, we will look at some of these opportunities.

BUSINESS AND DATA PROCESSING
APPLICATIONS PROGRAMMING

Business and data processing applications programmers work in business, finance, and manufacturing. They also work for software houses and computer service companies specializing in business data processing. These programmers design, code, test, and debug programs involving large quantities of data. They may help to design overall data processing systems and to organize the ways in which information is handled and processed within an organization. Banks and other financial institutions; accounting, real estate, and insurance firms; credit card companies; and personnel, payroll, and accounts departments of every kind of business: all are employers of business applications programmers.

Programmer-analyst. Many positions in business data processing are identified by the title, "programmer-analyst." This job title can mean different things in different companies. In small companies with small computers, "programmer-analyst" may be the main job category, even at the entry level. This reflects the fact that the "computer person" in a small installation may have to do just about everything related to the company's data processing system. This person will do routine programming. He or she will also design, maintain, and supervise all aspects of data processing operations.

In other situations, the title "programmer-analyst" represents the growing recognition on the part of businesses of the importance of systems analysis and systems operations: that is, getting the best software and making it work most effectively. This is especially true as more companies purchase their business applications software from commercial vendors, making changes or providing input to fit their own requirements. Since the main program is purchased from others, a company needs fewer in-house programmers to do basic programming tasks. What employers seek are programmer-analysts able to analyze data processing requirements, select the best available system, and make sure it works as well as possible. In business data processing today, systems analysis and systems optimization occupies a growing amount of the computer specialist's time.

Finally, in large companies, "programmer-analyst" may be little more than an indication of status: a level of promotion above the category of programmer.

Business data processing programmers and programmer-analysts do much of their work in COBOL. In 1983, COBOL, together with FORTRAN and assembly languages, accounted for 53 percent of all programming. In earlier years, business data processing was done exclusively in COBOL. The growth in the use of small business computers in the past few years has made other languages important. Today, BASIC, Pascal, and RPG II (a business-report generating language) are far more common on small commercial systems. Business applications for the most part involve processing accounting, inventory, sales, and payroll data. Business programmers may also develop or use sophisticated financial analysis and forecasting methods that chart company performance and predict future business trends.

Successful business applications programmers combine a knowledge of business data processing languages with a background in accounting, finance, or other business-related subjects. You do not need to know a lot about mathematics, but you should feel comfortable with numbers. Most business data processing involves a good deal of arithmetic and statistics. If you are considering this field, you should plan to take business courses in college and might want to consider a business minor. Indeed, many employers hire graduates with accounting or other business degrees who have a good knowledge of data processing and information systems. You might also want to consider a college major in management information systems (MIS) or systems sciences, rather than computer science. These degrees will be helpful if you wish to advance into data base management or other data processing management positions.

To do well in business applications, you need excellent interpersonal skills. You will often have to talk with people in many different departments of your company. You may have to instruct and supervise data entry clerks and operating personnel, if you work in smaller companies. And you will certainly have to provide management with the succinct, easily understandable reports they expect.

In business applications, you typically begin as a programmer-trainee or beginning programmer, if you work in a larger organization. You advance to chief or senior programmer, programmer-analyst, systems analyst, and into management of data processing operations. It is not unusual for successful individuals to move into company management positions. People begin as business applications programmers; for the most part, they do not remain at this level. But for the right kind of individual, business applications programming is an excellent place to start. More opportunities are available to business applications programmers and programmer-analysts than to any other group of computer professionals. And openings exist in virtually every industry.

SYSTEMS ANALYSIS

Systems analysts solve problems and design systems to improve the efficient handling of information, people, materials, and machines in business and industrial settings. The Association of Systems Management, the major professional organization in the field, defines systems analysis as

> . . . the process of reviewing the information and operational flows within an organization as a basis for service to management. It contributes to the optimal operation of the organization via two avenues: Information systems to provide timely, accurate, and meaningful information to management for use in decision making; and operating systems to accomplish specific organizational functions.

Systems analysts look at an area of a company's operations that is wasting time, causing trouble, or costing too much money. Using various analytical techniques, including cost accounting, sampling, interviewing, and computerized model buidling, they define the problem, come up with a solution, and report their proposed improvements to management. In this capacity, systems analysis is akin to operations research (see Chapter Five). While systems analysts work closely with computers, they are really systems, not computer, specialists. That is, they use their computer expertise to study and improve a department, process, or situation which they conceive of as a system, or interconnected series of conditions and events.

An example will help us better understand systems analysis. Let's say that a company would like to improve the way it deals with the information that flows through it each day. A systems analyst will see this flow of numbers, names, and words as an information management system. He or she will study current methods of dealing with this data. What information is needed? Who needs that information? Which employees are needed to handle this information? What kind of computer hardware and software is available? How much is the present information management system costing the company? And is it cost effective? The systems analyst will ask these and many other questions before arriving at an assessment of the system. Then he or she will design a different system to improve the efficiency and lower the cost of information processing. This might be a set of specifications describing appropriate software, input data, the way data is filed and stored in the computer system, and system output. It would also probably include the procedures or methods the data processing staff is to use in optimizing the system: getting it to perform as efficiently and economically as possible.

Systems analysts work in industrial and manufacturing environments as well as in business. In this sphere, a systems analyst is similar to an industrial engineer. For instance, a systems analyst may look at a factory and discover a problem in the flow of raw materials that is slowing down production. To solve this problem, the systems analyst would come up with a method to guarantee that enough materials are on hand to keep the plant operating at its most cost-effective level of productivity.

As you can see from these two examples, systems analysts are generalists. That means they may find themselves working in a variety of areas within an organization. They might work in accounting and finance departments, in administration, purchasing and inventory control, manufacturing and production, sales and marketing, even personnel management. But a large number of systems analysts work in data processing. To solve problems in manufacturing, a systems analyst must know something about production. To improve productivity in the payroll department, he or she will have to have some grasp of accounting. Systems analysts combine their knowledge of computer languages and systems with practical knowledge of the area in which they work. An ability to learn, a breadth of knowledge, and a store of practical experience are important keys to success in systems analysis.

A recent advertisement for a position with a large manufacturing company gives a good idea of the many facets of the systems analyst's job. The company was looking for an individual who could:

- write programs to process order, sales, billing, cash receipts, and sales reports and to forecast marketing trends;
- analyze business procedures and problems to refine data and convert it to programmable form for data processing;
- confer with heads of individual departments to determine their information needs;
- study existing data handling systems to evaluate data processing effectiveness;
- develop new systems to improve work flow and production;
- manage projects, assist in writing proposals, perform feasibility and cost analysis studies.

The majority of systems analysts are employed by manufacturing and processing, banks, financial or insurance organizations. Some work for data processing service firms, although as more businesses install their own computer systems, employment with these companies will decline. Systems analysts also work for public utility and transportation companies and for the federal government.

What kind of education does systems analysis require? Systems analysts must be familiar with programming languages, computer concepts, systems analysis techniques, and data retrieval techniques. Preferably, they have an undergraduate degree in computer science, information systems, or data processing. A few colleges offer undergraduate degrees in systems analysis. Some systems analysts have a degree in business supported by significant college coursework in computer science. Additional training in finance, banking, insurance, or other fields related to the kind of company for which the systems analyst works is considered desirable. For this reason, many systems analysts complete a fifth year of study beyond their bachelor's degree in a business-related subject. In systems analysis, an M.B.A. can be an asset.

Few if any individuals will begin their career as systems analysts. Most systems analysts begin as programmers, advance to programmer-analysts, and are promoted to systems analysts after some time on the job. This may take several years. Indeed, most systems analysts are over 30 years of age and have been employed in computer-related positions for a number of years. This experience gives them a good understanding of the overall functioning of their organization. This overview is necessary if the systems analyst is to see company operations as a system of interdependent units.

As we will see again in Chapter Eight, the employment outlook for systems analysts is exceptionally good. Systems analysis ranks thirteenth out of 240 professions in estimated growth potential. With a 1982 median salary of nearly $30,000, it is clear that systems analysts are also wellpaid professionals. Twenty-five percent of those responding to a survey by the Association for Systems Management reported a 1982 salary of more than $40,000.

As well as being wellpaid, systems analysts have many opportunities for advancement. Senior and lead systems analysts work with clients and management; they supervise other systems analysis staff as well as programmers and other data processing personnel. They may advance to become manager of systems analysis, supervising all systems-related projects within an organization. Advancement into data processing or information systems management is also possible. These management positions can lead to the highest levels of company responsibility.

Advancement in systems analysis is based on an individual's ongoing education in the latest data processing and resource management techniques. In-house training, seminars and special courses offered by computer vendors and professional organizations, and reading professional publications help the systems analyst to stay informed about new developments. Success in systems analysis demands a high level of professional commitment.

EDP AUDITOR

EDP (electronic data processing) auditors are the watchdogs of large data processing systems. EDP auditors help their companies reduce current financial losses attributable to data processing operations and guard against future losses. Working in banks, large public accounting firms, and other financially-based businesses, EDP auditors assess computer systems and data processing procedures to locate any possiblity of loss and evaluate the degree of risk involved.

EDP auditors locate irregularities, errors, and fraud in data processing systems. These errors may be something as simple as a data entry clerk's input mistakes or system malfunctions caused by a spilled cup of coffee. Errors of a graver nature are the EDP auditor's target as well. Unacceptable accounting methods, unauthorized access to computer files, or outright fraud are detected and reported to upper management.

About three-fourths of an EDP auditor's time is spent collecting information. The auditor interviews data processing personnel, administers questionnaires to system users, checks the computer programs to find errors or potential problems in coding, and verifies that all information on file is correct and up-to-date. Other duties may include advising management in the selection of a data processing system or special software package to suit company needs, testing new systems to make sure everything is working reliably, and writing programs to audit the system. The EDP auditor is like a police detective; he or she makes sure that no one is siphoning off a few cents here or there into a private account.

Clearly, an EDP auditor must be able to program well and must fully understand computer operations. He or she will have a broad background in business applications programming, and will have worked on a variety of systems. In addition, he or she must understand accounting and financial practices and keep up-to-date on the latest EDP auditing techniques.

Communication and interpersonal skills are exceedingly important to an EDP auditor. He or she must often report unpleasant facts to upper management and has to be able to talk with programmers, accountants, and data processing personnel about what they do without arousing their defensiveness or antagonism.

To become an EDP auditor, you need an undergraduate degree in computer science or in business with considerable computer coursework. You also usually need at least two years' experience in the design, programming, and operations of large business systems. An M.B.A. degree or certification as a CPA (Certified Public Accountant) is an added qualification.

A position as EDP auditor offers motivated individuals who have advanced to senior programmer or systems analyst positions an opportunity to move into management. Work in EDP auditing can lead to higher-level corporate management or to consulting.

POSITIONS IN MANAGEMENT

Promotion and advancement from the positions we have described in this and in the previous chapter lead to management. But just what does a *manager* do? We are so used to hearing the term "manager" applied to everyone from the shift supervisor of the local fast-food chain to senior corporate executives that we sometimes lose sight of the actual work a manager does.

We can distinguish two kinds of managerial responsibility: responsibility for people and financial responsibility. A manager supervises others. This is the principal meaning we give to the word, management, in the computer or any other industry. A manager may also allocate resources and facilities. At higher levels especially, managers are executives who have a budget and whose decisions affect the profit and loss of their company or corporation. Generally speaking, the higher the level of management, the greater the manager's financial responsiblity, and the more effect his or her decisions will have on company profitability.

As you can see, then, the individual in a computer-related career who wishes to reach these higher levels of achievement will almost certainly need to know a good deal about business. A solid technical background is not enough. Of course, much practical business knowledge is gained from actual work experience. It is important to realize, though, that at some point in their careers, most computer specialists have to choose between a narrowly technical focus and the wider (but not always as technically satisfying) opportunities of working with people and money as well as with systems and machines.

In the following pages, we will look at a representative range of computer-related managerial positions.

Project Management

Project managers coordinate all aspects of a specific hardware or software development project. These individuals plan, direct, and supervise the efforts of the project team. They schedule work and write progress reports. They also serve as a link between the project team and other divisions and departments.

Project managers need the technical background and experience that will enable them to assist in project development. In addition, successful project managers have exceptional interpersonal skills. This job requires working closely with a limited number of technical people and non-technical support staff. It is up to the project manager to maintain group harmony and productivity.

Promotion to project manager comes from senior programming positions. Project managers have no or limited financial responsibility. They remain in close contact with technical developments. Indeed, this is the most technically-oriented managerial position of any we describe.

The project manager position can be a stepping stone to higher echelons of management. In larger vendor organizations, project management also provides a niche for the technically-minded individual more interested in bits and bytes than in profit and loss.

Data Base Management

The data base specialist builds and maintains a large, cross-referenced library of computerized information using a special kind of software, called a "data base management system" (DBMS). A data base can integrate a number of separate files, making information instantaneously available to users. For instance, in a large health clinic, a variety of information must be kept on each patient. The clinic keeps records on personal statistics: the patient's name, address, date of birth, marital status, number of children, and so on. The billing department needs to know the patient's name and address, as well as all visits to clinic physicians and the charges for those visits and other services. The dermatologist needs records of the patient's visits to the office, diagnoses, and treatments. He or she may need to know that the patient visited the allergist two years ago for treatment of a skin rash, but does not want to have to deal with information on billing and payments for that visit. If each department or doctor maintained separate files, much information would be unnecessarily duplicated. This would take considerable computer memory space. Moreover, if each user of the system had to extract the information on, for instance, visits to the allergist from facts on all other aspects of the patient's records, much time would be wasted.

The data base specialist designs a software system to combine these records into a single, efficient data structure (or system of files), and makes sure that each department can quickly retrieve just the information it needs. In other words, the data base specialist is a kind of "resource policeman," managing information and making sure the data base is both usable to and useful for those who need it. In smaller organizations, the data base manager (sometimes called a "data base administrator") may have no staff or budget. In larger operations, a data base manager may supervise other data base programming specialists and will work within a budget allocated for information management.

Data base specialists get information to users who need it; they also keep users from retrieving confidential or classified data. In some installations, data base specialists may be in charge of overall computer security.

The demand for data base specialists is expected to grow, especially in conjunction with the growth of complex communications systems linking computers and telecommunications equipment and with the rise of distributed data processing using these networks. Data base specialists work in large user organizations with mainframe data processing centers. They are also employed by computer service companies, in smaller distributed data processing facilities, and in consulting.

To become a data base manager, you need several years of technical and business data processing experience and an expert knowledge of data structures, programming languages, and operating systems. Advances in expert systems may create a new kind of information manager, responsible for constructing and maintaining dynamic knowledge bases. At this point, the "resource policeman" becomes a knowledge engineer.

Manager, Management Information Systems

The MIS manager is an executive who spends most of his or her time directing all aspects of information systems and data processing within an organization. Advancing from systems and data base management positions, the MIS manager hires and supervises systems and applications programmers, systems analysts, and other data processing personnel. He or she assesses overall information processing needs and makes recommendations for system improvements. The MIS manager is principally responsible for budgeting for data processing staff and operations. He or she writes proposals and reports concerning improved systems operations and answers to high-level management.

The MIS management position is itself at a high level within an organization. Achievement of this position represents many years of management experience. And although most information systems managers start their careers as programmers, by the time they arrive at this level of management, very little of their time is spent in direct computing activities.

In larger organizations, an individual is promoted to MIS manager after gaining considerable experience in systems management. Because decisions made in the way information is handled and processed can have dramatic effects on a company's productivity, the MIS manager must know a good deal about the particular industry in which he or she works. Large organizations look for job candidates with technical and business skills and tend to favor the candidate with an M.B.A.

Smaller organizations offer more immediate opportunities to advance into MIS management. Systems analysts or programming managers can advance into this position as a small company expands its computing operations, facilities, and personnel. In these smaller companies, MIS management may be synonymous with data processing management. In large corporate environments, the MIS manager may supervise a data processing manager with more limited responsibilities.

Decision Support Services

Decision support systems (DSS) are an emerging class of computer applications. DSS uses computer tools, including data base and DSS software, to assist business executives in decision-making. Growing out of operations research (see Chapter Five), these systems apply statistical modeling and analysis techniques to various business problems, including financial planning and forecasting, marketing strategies, and manpower allocations.

Decision support services departments are relatively new. Many DSS functions overlap with management information systems, and many DSS personnel work in MIS departments. In companies where a separate DSS department does exist, it is usually parallel to or a part of the MIS department. Implemented through telecommunications and computer networks, DSS make it possible for an executive to obtain information and make decisions from terminal locations around the globe.

What are the decision support services manager's duties? Like the MIS manager, he or she supervises a staff of lower-level managers, programmers, and analysts. He or she may be in charge of financial modeling and decision analyses for a company. His or her department may direct other facets of information management systems as well.

MARKETING AND MARKETING SUPPORT

Marketing Representatives

Marketing representatives sell computer hardware, software, and systems. They work for vendors selling mainframes, small general-purpose computers, and special-purpose computer systems for office or manufacturing automation. They sell software packages and peripheral equipment like printers, terminals, and telecommunications interfaces. The marketing representative links vendor and user, matching user needs with vendor products.

As the cost of computer equipment has declined and the range of applications has been extended, so has the need for marketing representatives increased. In 1983 alone, one large vendor, NCR, planned to add 500 people to its sales force, recruiting college graduates with a computer science or related technical degree.

To become a marketing representative, you need a thorough understanding of computer hardware, software, systems, and applications. You must also be able to judge the user's needs to provide an appropriate system. Sometimes the user organization will know what their computing requirements are. Sometimes, the marketing representative must start from scratch, working with a client who may know little about computers to define computing needs and select an acceptable product. Thus, the marketing representative depends on his or her communications skills. Oral communication skills are particularly important, as the marketing representative often makes informational and sales presentations, and must talk easily with clients. In addition, the marketing representative must be energetic, highly motivated, and willing to travel. Most computer sales occur at the user's company. The marketing representative travels to these locations to demonstrate a system or make a sale. And most marketing representatives work on a quota system. This means they are responsible for making a certain number of sales within a limited period of time.

Above all else, the successful marketing representative must have a certain flair for sales. One industry recruiting expert describes this as a "sales personality," difficult to define, but clearly recognizable. Computer sales does not, however, employ stereotypical high-pressure sales tactics. Marketing representatives in the computer industry believe in their product and can back up their belief with technical knowledge. Large sales may be the result of bids or proposals prepared by the vendor and its marketing representatives in response to specifications supplied by the purchasing organization. Most clients spend a considerable amount of money to purchase computing systems; they are paying in part for the expertise of the sales personnel. Moreover, clients are sometimes highly sophisticated computer users and expect marketing representatives to spell out in detail all technical features of the products they are selling.

Education varies among marketing representatives, though most jobs with larger vendors require a college degree. Some engineering-oriented vendors, especially those that sell to technically sophisticated users, prefer to hire people with a computer science or engineering degree, if they show sales potential. At present, the demand for sales personnel with technical training in microcomputers and telecommunications interfaces is especially high.

Other companies look for individuals with a marketing or other degree and some evidence that they can deal effectively with the technical features of the products they will represent. Some college programs provide training in technical marketing and sales.

In either case, a company's sales force will be exhaustively trained in company products. And training is an ongoing part of the marketing representative's job, as new products are developed or present products modified.

Marketing representatives generally move into marketing or general management positions. *Marketing managers* supervise the sales force of marketing representatives. They direct the sales operations for a particular geographical region or handle one or more special client accounts. A degree in computer science combined with marketing and sales experience and an M.B.A. is a virtually certain ticket into executive positions. Marketing representatives also may find opportunities to move into managerial positions with user companies. Having worked to supply the best system for the user, they have learned the user's computing needs from the inside out. This knowledge and their experience with the system that they sell makes such individuals attractive employees to user organizations.

Sales opportunities also exist with retail computer stores. Most of these positions do not require a college degree in computer science; many may not require a college degree at all. Management of retail computer stores takes more specialized computer training combined with business education. These are low-level positions, however, without many avenues of professional development or advancement.

Marketing Technical Support Representatives

Marketing technical support representatives provide a liason between a vendor's sales force and the organization purchasing the vendor's system. *Systems engineers* focus on software problems, while *field* or *customer engineers* specialize in hardware. Before a sale, marketing technical support personnel evaluate a customer's computing needs. They demonstrate equipment and software, help to write sales proposals, and generally assist the marketing representative to deliver the system that best meets the client's specifications. After a sale, technical support representatives install the system and get it up and running. Their responsibilities do not end here, however. Technical support representatives continue to serve as consultants to their clients. They may train users, resolve problems that arise in day-to-day use of the system, and function as troubleshooters. When something goes wrong, the user contacts the systems engineer for help. IBM pioneered the idea of such continuing customer service and has set the standard for marketing and product support for the entire computer industry.

Marketing technical support representatives are salaried members of a vendor's technical staff. Unlike marketing representatives, they do not work on a commission or quota basis. Clearly, though, these individuals play an important role in the sales function. While the sales force may sell the system, the marketing technical support representatives make sure it does what it is supposed to do. The reputation of a vendor is often based on the adequacy of its technical support.

Most vendors prefer to hire technical support representatives who have a four-year computer science or related technical degree, although some marketing personnel may move into this area if they develop enough skill in handling technical problems. Technical support representatives must be flexible enough to learn about the clients' businesses in order to understand their computing needs. And because so much of a technical support representative's job involves talking with their customers and giving presentations, excellent oral communication skills are necessary, as well as the ability to adapt to the user's environment.

Marketing technical support representatives usually undergo extensive training in their company's hardware and software systems, and in other subjects important in developing workable user systems, such as networking and telecommunications. This training will involve marketing techniques and communications strategies as well. After training, a systems engineer will be assigned a number of client accounts, and spends most of his or her time at customer locations. Field engineers are called in on an as-needed basis.

A company's clearest "personality" and expertise is reflected in its marketing technical support staff. These positions offer a chance for the individual who wishes to work with people as well as with systems. And work in technical support offers the immediate reward of seeing the usefulness of your work when you help your client to use your system effectively.

Advancement opportunities from technical support lead in either management or technical directions. From technical support, some people will move into sales, and advance to manage marketing and technical support activities. Others, who enjoy the technical challenges of this job, will advance to advisory, senior, or consulting levels in systems and customer engineering.

TWO CAREER PROFILES

Systems Engineer, Marketing Technical Support

Cindy graduated three years ago with a B.S. in computer science and went to work for IBM as a systems engineer. In looking for a job, she felt she wanted to do something that would bring her in contact with people. She didn't want to spend all day sitting alone at her desk. Systems engineering, the technical side of marketing at IBM, offered her this opportunity.

Her first year at IBM was spent in intensive training. She was assigned to an advisor in a branch office location of the company's marketing division, and worked with her advisor on small projects in order to gain experience with customers. At the same time, she completed self-study modules which prepared her for more formal episodes of training. These self-study courses covered technical subjects including virtual storage concepts, distributed networks, and systems programming, all related to IBM hardware and software. Cindy was also becoming familiar with IBM equipment.

Every six to eight weeks during this year, Cindy was sent to three- to four-week formal training courses, returning each time to her branch office. This training included lectures on technical subjects and exercises designed to help her practice making sales calls and presentations. Cindy recalls that these training episodes were not unlike the kind of work she had done in college. And she also remembers her reluctance at speaking before others. She vowed to complete her training without ever giving an oral sales presentation before the other trainees. Of course, she didn't manage to avoid this training in oral presentation skills. And as a result of this training, Cindy has become a confident and effective spokesperson for IBM equipment and systems.

Today, Cindy manages seven customer accounts. Most of her days are spent away from her home office at customer sites. Like other technical support professionals, she has developed a "home" in each of her customer companies, and visits each at least once a week.

Cindy's responsibilities include systems implementation and maintenance. She makes sure her customers have a system that can handle their computing needs. When customers have a problem or need a special application, Cindy advises them on IBM products that could be useful to them. Her main job is to keep their systems running smoothly. She deals only with software problems, however.

When a hardware problem comes up, she calls on IBM's customer engineers.

Although she works, as she puts it, "in the trenches" with her clients, she is not, like a marketing representative, paid on commission. She sums up her relation to the sales force: "The marketing representative makes the promises. We try to make it happen."

Cindy enjoys the many benefits of working for a large corporation. She sees many possibilities for advancement in both technical and management directions. IBM, she feels, has a basic "respect for the individual" and encourages an attitude that each employee is important in his or her own right. Because of this emphasis on individual worth and accomplishment, Cindy believes IBM is a very good place for a woman. Employees are treated equally and without bias; advancement is based solely on ability.

Cindy enjoys her work tremendously. "I was interested in being technical, but not in being a programmer," she says. Her work as a systems engineer lets her use her technical knowledge and her skills with people. The pace of her job can get hectic: "I never run out of things to do and people to talk to." And IBM's position on the leading edge of new technology and product development means she never stops learning. As a new product comes out, she is one of the first to understand it and make it work for her customers.

For students interested in a computer career, Cindy agrees with other professionals in the importance of gaining practical work experience. She advises students to search out any kind of part-time or summer "hands-on" experience as an operator or programmer. When she arrived at IBM with her degree in computing science, Cindy recalls "I couldn't load a tape drive to save my life," adding that it is hard to convince your customers that you know what you are talking about if you haven't mastered such simple mechanical tasks. Moreover, work experience looks good on your resume.

Cindy also suggests that a minor in electrical engineering would be a useful complement to the software emphasis of many undergraduate programs in computer science. Coursework in electrical engineering "let's you know how a computer works, from the inside out, and you cease to see it as a black box," capable of infinite magic. Cindy's own undergraduate training emphasized programming skills. She feels that this helped her to "think like a computer—in a logical way," but points out that there is much more to computers and computing than FORTRAN and BASIC. "Everything today is communications, data bases, networking," she concludes. "If I had to do it over, I'd take tougher courses in computer *science*," not just programming.

Data Processing/MIS Manager

Bob is the information systems manager for a small oil and gas exploration and production company with fifteen years' experience in the computer field. He got into computing, he says, by accident. Bob majored in accounting in college. One day, one of his accounting professors assigned a lab which required some programming. And that was it: Bob "fell in love" with programming. Completing that assignment led Bob to a part-time programming job while he was still in school. And although he went on to complete his degree in accounting, he's been in the computer field ever since.

Bob's is the classic career path. Once out of school, he was hired as an entry-level programmer. He advanced through the senior programmer level to become a systems analyst, then moved up into data processing management. Along the way, he obtained an M.B.A. to increase his knowledge of management techniques. He has stayed in the oil and gas industry throughout his career, working for oil field equipment as well as oil and gas production companies.

Because Bob works for a younger, smaller company, he was solely responsible for setting up the entire information handling installation. To do this, he interviewed top management to ascertain their information requirements and the overall company direction, in order to develop a system that would meet start-up as well as future needs. He supervised installation of the system and continues to maintain and improve it. He hires (and fires, he adds) systems and applications programmers and programmer/analysts, and oversees the information processing department. About 80 percent of system processing involves general maintenance of company operations: payroll, accounting, general ledger, financial planning, and—because his company owns or leases oil-producing lands—software that keeps up-to-date land management records. The remaining 20 percent of company computing is devoted to processing seismic information, well logging, and other geological data related to oil exploration.

A good deal of Bob's time and energy is spent on budgeting for his department: a task, he points out, that is never over. He also helps to acquire, install, and maintain new software systems as company information processing needs evolve. He spends hours on the telephone or in meetings, and admits that while he gains considerable personal and professional satisfaction from his management position, "frankly, programming is more fun."

Bob advises students in computer science to think twice about aiming for management positions. "Bit twiddlers" and "byte benders," people who are really excited by low-level programming and the machine, may not enjoy being a manager. Such people will probably be happier and more productive remaining in a purely technical or engineering environment as a systems programmer, project leader, or in scientific and engineering applications.

In hiring, Bob likes "to find the people that discover by accident that they have a flair for computing." He looks for young people who "like to play with computers" but also have some knowledge of business "because they can talk with users." Bob sums up his advice to people considering a career in computers:

> Go to college and don't quit until you're through. At least get your bachelor's degree. And try to get some practical experience during college. It's extremely difficult to break into the field as a programmer-trainee. Only the very big companies can afford to train people.

This Systems Research Laboratory SRL 1000 IV computerized pulmonary function laboratory is used for patient testing at Ingalls Hospital in Harvey, Illinois. Photo: Gould Inc.

CHAPTER 5

SPECIAL OPPORTUNITIES IN COMPUTER-RELATED FIELDS

There are an ever-increasing number of career opportunities in computer-related fields. We cannot begin in this book to review them all. In this chapter, however, we examine a few of these opportunities.

DOCUMENTATION: TECHNICAL WRITERS

Technical writers combine a knowledge of computer science (or other scientific or technical field) with an ability to write effectively. In the computer industry, technical writers provide *documentation:* reference and users' manuals and other documents that support and explain computer systems and software. Documentation helps the user, who may know little about computers, to understand, operate, and program the machine. Documentation also enables computer scientists to understand the purpose of another expert's code.

Many fields, including aerospace, manufacturing, and government, as well as all areas of engineering, need individuals who can communicate specialized information to many different types of reader. Because of the recent growth of computer use in the workplace and the home, writers of computer documentation are in considerable demand.

People who begin as technical writers may advance into

managerial or administrative positions directing a technical writing group or publications department and coordinating document production.

Employers are always eager to hire individuals with good communications skills. In a competitive job market, the applicant who can communicate effectively has a clear advantage. If you would like to combine your interest in computer science with technical writing, you should take as many courses in journalism and English composition as you can. Courses in technical writing and editing and in publications production are especially recommended. The Society for Technical Communication (815 15th Street, N.W., Suite 506, Washington, DC 20005) is the professional organization for technical writers and documentation specialists. The STC is a good source for additional information on this subject.

EDUCATION

Many opportunities in computer science education exist within private industry and in public and private schools at all levels.

Vendors of computer equipment and software employ instructors to conduct in-house training and to teach those who purchase their products how to use them. For many vendors, customer training is central to their sales effort.

In-house company course instructors lead seminars and training sessions for employees. These individuals often have advanced technical knowledge and the ability to share it with others. Customer training personnel combine their technical know-how with well-developed interpersonal skills. Oral communication and teaching abilities may be more important in customer training than advanced training in computer science. Thus these individuals may not hold college degrees in computer science. They may move into customer training from technical writing, marketing, or sales positions.

Depending on the company and its customers, training positions may require considerable travel. Certainly, to do well in customer training, you must enjoy helping others to master basic aspects of computer use.

Many companies have an educational services department or division. In addition to coordinating all aspects of company training programs, this division may produce instructional materials such as self-paced computer programming tutorials, instruction guides, videocassettes, or films.

In public and private education, opportunities to teach students how to use computers exist at both elementary and secondary levels. Many public school districts hire tutors or consultants to assist them in bringing computers into their classrooms. In many schools, computer programming is already an established part of the curriculum. And through computer-aided instruction (CAI), the computer can become a tool for teaching other subjects. CAI software has been written to teach everything from elementary arithmetic and spelling to fairly advanced courses in engineering fundamentals. Instructional software has also been commercially successful with home computer users.

At the college and university level, the shortage of qualified computer science professors is severe. Three factors have brought about this shortage: the rapid growth in the number of computer science departments and degree programs, increases in student enrollments, and the fact that, on the whole, qualified individuals can make more money in industry than they can at the university. As a consequence, most computer science departments are hard-pressed to meet their staffing needs.

If college teaching is not as financially rewarding as working in industry, it offers satisfactions of other sorts. College instructors introduce students to the field of computer science, encourage their interest, and help to educate them to become productive professionals. They teach students from a variety of majors to understand how computers work and how they influence society. In addition to their teaching, professors conduct research and publish their results. For many, the chance to do research is extremely important. And many professors of computer science supplement their incomes through consulting. The flexible schedule of the university gives them time for research and consulting.

College instructors must hold graduate degrees. A Ph.D. is preferred, although because of the present demand, many instructors are employed with just their Master's.

MEDICINE

The potential for computer applications in medicine is extraordinary. At present, neither the nature nor extent of all that computers might be able to do in medicine is fully known. There is considerable potential for growth in straightforward data processing applications: billing, patient records, the day-to-day record keeping of a hospital or clinic. A major problem of most hospitals is making sure their bills are paid. The cost and quality of health care affects us all, and the pressure to keep costs under control is great. Automating medical records and billing can tremendously improve health care productivity.

However, data processing is not the only or most interesting way computers are used in medicine. Data base networks provide physicians with instant access to information on poisons, rare diseases, and accident treatment. Even more intriguing possiblities exist in the development of expert systems that incorporate the knowledge of a doctor's lifetime medical practice. One such system, CADUCEUS, jointly developed by a physician and a computer scientist, diagnoses disorders and diseases in internal medicine. Another more specialized system, MYCIN, diagnoses blood and meningitis infections and suggests treatment methods to the attending physician. These systems not only assist experienced doctors and nurses, but may someday be used by medical practitioners in rural or remote locations where doctors are not available.

Computers have even been used in the area of mental health. One program, ELIZA, introduced as long ago as 1967, asks patients questions about their feelings, registers the pattern of words in the patients' responses, then forms new questions that are based on those responses. This feedback technique has proved remarkably successful: many people find it easier to express their troubles and anxieties to a computer that to a human therapist.

Bioengineering, engineering applied to develop sophisticated technology to test and treat health problems, also relies increasingly on computer technology. We are all already familiar with simple devices like digital thermometers and blood testing equipment. In the future, computer science and engineering, bioengineering, genetics engineering, and robotics will combine in ways that even the most imaginative science fiction writer cannot conceive of today.

Both the Association for Computing Machinery and the IEEE Computer Society have special interest groups for medical computing. The American Association for Medical Systems and Informatics is also concerned with medical computing.

INFORMATION SCIENCE

Information scientists use their knowledge of mathematics, computer science, and data processing techniques to design large information storage and retrieval systems. These systems let users obtain specific information from computer storage easily, quickly, and reliably. For instance, a geologist doing research on earthquake activity in Southern California can instruct these systems to locate all information published on this subject in the past five years. The rapid expansion in human knowledge made possible by the computer has made information science a field of considerable importance.

Information scientists develop methods to collect, organize, and classify information for computer storage and retrieval. They then construct, maintain, and update the system they have designed. Information scientists often specialize in particular fields, such as agriculture, medicine, education, or chemistry. This is because they must have some understanding of the information to be classified. Automated searches of stored information are done using key words or descriptors. Thus, the system must be designed and key words selected according to the logic of the field itself.

Information science is closely related to library science, for these large information systems are really vast electronic libraries. Information scientists are employed wherever there are large quantities of information to be organized. Employers include commercial data banks and computerized information services, large corporations, and government agencies.

The American Society for Information Science has prepared a booklet giving more details about careers in this field.

OPERATIONS RESEARCH

Operations research, also known as decision or management science, applies scientific principles to decision-making. The OR specialist analyzes a problem, then uses the computer to mathematically or statistically model (or simulate) the effects of alternate decisions. By so doing he or she seeks to discover the most suitable course of action. OR is used to determine how best to design, operate, or manage systems to optimize the allocation of resources and people.

Today, OR specialists solve problems in production management, optimize computer networks and telecommunications systems, and design mass transit systems. They work with man-machine interface problems, automation and robotics, land use and highway planning, financial planning and forecasting, medical decision making, meteorology, ecology, and in many, many other areas of modern life.

Whether their subject is a hospital, a company, a production line, or an electrical power grid, OR specialists view things as a *system*. When applied to manufacturing and automation, OR is a tool of industrial engineering. While similar in many ways to (and often overlapping with) systems analysis, OR is distinguished by its heavy reliance on mathematics and statistics, modeling, and computer simulation.

By its very nature, operations research is an interdisciplinary field. OR analysts hold undergraduate degrees in many different disciplines. However, all OR specialists have a strong quantitative background, including courses in probability and statistics, linear algebra, economics, and, of course, computer science. Some colleges offer undergraduate degrees in operations research or management science; some programs in industrial engineering, systems analysis, or management emphasize OR methods. However, most work in operations research requires graduate study. Typically, a student with an undergraduate degree in math, computer science, management, or engineering will go on to specialized graduate study in OR.

The Operations Research Society of America has prepared a booklet, "Career Opportunities in Operations Research," that more fully describes employment opportunities in this field.

INDUSTRIAL ENGINEERING

In industrial engineering, computers are used to improve manufacturing efficiency. Computer applications include numerical control, computer-aided design and manufacture, and robotics.

Numerical control machines have been in use since the 1950's and are very common today. These are machines like a lathe, dedicated to a single manufacturing task and driven by a computer program commonly stored on paper tape. One of the early recognized advantages of numerical control was the ease with which manufacturing specifications could be changed by changing the computer program, instead of resetting the machine by hand. This saved time and labor and increased the flexibility of the production line.

More recently, computer-aided design and manufacturing (CAD/CAM) have received wide attention. Computer-aided design (CAD) relies on very high-power, high-resolution graphics terminals and software that allow engineers to draw a part or product design on the video screen. This eliminates time-consuming drafting and redrafting of various stages of the design. When the design is perfected, it can be printed out directly by a plotter (a graphics output device similar to a printer). CAD applications have been widely adopted in the automotive and electronics industries, as well as by architects and other designers.

Computer-aided manufacture (CAM) uses a hierarchy of computers to control many facets of the production process. At the lowest level, process control computers perform separate tasks in

More and more types of businesses are becoming computer-related. Photo:
Texas Instruments Data Systems Group.

the production sequence. At a higher level, large micro- or minicomputers monitor and direct the entire operation. Ideally, in fully integrated computer-aided manufacture (CIM or ICAM), CAD programs will be directly "down-loaded" to lower level computers and operations research models will automatically optimize the production system from design to end-product.

The most highly publicized element of CAD/CAM is undoubtedly robotics. Robots, for all the mystique the word evokes, are really just extremely flexible computer-controlled machines. A numerically controlled machine can be programmed to different specifications, but it can still only perform one task. A robot, on the other hand, can be programmed to manipulate a range of tools or to perform a number of different tasks.

Robots are programmed using specialized "geometrical" languages that instruct them to move from point A to point B. Because the robot cannot deviate from these instructions, the workplace has to be set up with great precision. Parts must be located exactly where the robot has been programmed to expect them. If a part is even slightly out of alignment, the robot cannot "find" it.

This problem could be solved if robots could be programmed to see or feel, to recognize shapes, and to adjust to differing conditions. To do this, industrial engineers and computer scientists are working to develop robot sensations, especially vision. So far, limited results have been achieved. But the day when robots have anything approaching human vision is some distance in the future.

Industrial engineering and robotics offer many attractive career opportunities. People will be needed to design the manufacturing tasks that robots will perform, to design the workplace in which they operate, and to program the machines. If you are interested in engineering applications of computer technology and have some mechanical inclinations, you might consider industrial engineering as a career option. The Society of Manufacturing Engineers has a strong student program. This group can give you furthur information about industrial engineering, CAD/CAM, and robotics.

Courses in computer science taken in high school, college, or trade school can help a person find a job. Photo: Bell & Howell Education Group.

CHAPTER 6

EDUCATION

You do not need a college education to perform many jobs in computer operations and maintenance. However, professional-level positions in the computer field increasingly require completion of a four-year degree at a recognized college or university.

Nor do you need to major in computer science to find challenging work in the field of computing. There are two reasons for this. First, until fairly recently, formal academic programs in computer science did not exist. Twenty-five years ago, you could not major in computer science. As recently as 1970-71, only 2,388 bachelor's degrees in computer and information sciences were awarded in a single academic year. Many individuals employed today entered the field in its infancy. They learned how to use computers in the course of their everyday occupations as mathematicians, scientists, or engineers.

Second, because computers have such a wide range of applications in so many different areas, many individuals combine study in science, engineering, or business disciplines with a secondary concentration on the uses of computers in their major field.

However, as the profession matures, an undergraduate degree in computer science will become the standard certification for entry into many positions, especially those with a technical or systems emphasis. Indeed, this is essentially true today. And as more and more students enter the job market with computer science degrees, competition is becoming increasingly fierce. Many employers can already choose from among a number of graduates, and will prefer candidates with outstanding grades, related work experience, or graduate study.

In the following pages, we will examine educational programs in computer science and discuss what steps you can take to ensure that you receive sound preparation for a successful, productive career.

HIGH SCHOOL

If you are still in high school, what can you do to begin to prepare for a career in computer science? We can give you four points of advice:

1. Follow a solid college-preparatory course of studies with an emphasis on mathematics and English.
2. Learn as much as you can about computers and computing.
3. Develop good study habits.
4. Begin planning for college as early in your high school career as possible.

It is never too early in your high school studies to begin to plan for college. By the end of your junior year, you should be making concrete plans for your college education. If you have decided that computer science is attractive to you, you will want to read the following sections in this book on selecting a college. Choose four or five colleges you think you might like to attend and write for copies of their catalogs, admission requirements, housing, financial aid, and other information. Most schools require students to submit their results on the Scholastic Apptitude Test (SAT) or the American College Test (ACT). These tests are offered at a limited number of locations several times each year. You need to arrange to take them in advance.

In addition to these standardized tests of academic achievement and ability, many colleges and universities have other admission requirements. You may need to have taken so many credit hours in English, social science, science, math, or foreign languages. Some schools will also ask you to write an essay explaining your reasons for seeking admission to their school, to visit their campus to be interviewed by a campus admissions officer, or to provide letters of recommendation.

If you are planning to go to college, you should be enrolled in a college preparatory program in high school. Your coursework should include solid training in mathematics, especially if you are interested in the theoretical or engineering aspects of computers and computer science. Physics is also recommended. Good communications skills will be crucial to your success in college and beyond. Take as many English courses as you can, especially those which emphasize writing. And a course in public speaking or speech communication will improve your confidence and self-expression, helping you to communicate effectively with others.

Of course, take every opportunity to learn as much as you can about computers and computing. If your high school offers courses in programming, by all means take them. If your school has a computer club, you will certainly want to become a member. Learning about computers is not limited to school, however. Many computer stores have classes in BASIC and other subjects geared to the systems they sell. Many of these courses are especially aimed at high school students. Try to get experience with languages other than BASIC, though. BASIC will teach you programming habits you will have to break when you take more advanced programming courses.

If your family owns a microcomputer, or if you have other access to a machine, you can increase your computer knowledge by writing original programs for it. Also, microcomputer users' clubs abound. Participation in these loosely-organized groups of enthusiasts will contribute to your computer knowledge. While microcomputer experience will be very different from the mainframe courses you will have in college, your familiarity with general computer vocabulary and procedures will be an undeniable advantage to you.

Admission to better colleges and universities requires good grades. A record of solid academic achievement will increase the likelihood of your acceptance by the college of your choice. Development of good study habits and a commitment to perform at the peak of your ability will encourage your academic success in high school. And good study habits and self-discipline will be essential in college. Writing and debugging programs, learning about computer science theory and practice, demand concentration, patience, attention to detail—and time. If you cannot discipline yourself to study intensely, to set aside significant amounts of study time and use that time effectively, you stand little chance of doing well in college. Each year, numbers of college freshmen fail to make it to their sophomore year because they failed to develop good study habits while in high school.

TWO-YEAR JUNIOR AND COMMUNITY COLLEGES

Many two-year junior and community colleges offer associate degrees in computer science, computer programming, and data processing. An associate degree may help you to obtain a lower-level data processing position or a good job as a computer maintenance and repair technician. However, most professional-level positions in computing now require a four-year college degree.

Many students choose for financial or personal reasons to attend a junior or community college for two years and then transfer to a recognized four-year school. For many students, this is a good way to smooth the transition from high school to the more competitive, less-sheltered university environment. It can also help students who decide fairly late in high school that obtaining a college education is important. A year or two at a junior college can give you time to improve your study habits and your grades and may better prepare you for more advanced study in computer science.

If you decide, for whatever reason, to attend a two-year college and to transfer later to a four-year school, it is important to follow a general course of study that will satisfy the requirements of the college or university to which you wish to transfer. Be careful to take a wide range of general requirements. A narrow emphasis on computer or other technical courses may jeopardize your admission to the college of your choice. Also, many colleges and universities will not accept all credits transferred from another school. This is especially true of requirements in your major field. You will cause yourself fewest problems and potential disappointments if you discuss in advance entrance requirements and transfer policies with admissions officers from your chosen four-year school. Then plan your junior college curriculum to meet those requirements.

FOUR-YEAR COLLEGES AND UNIVERSITIES

Selecting a College or University

In selecting a college or university, you should be guided by a number of considerations.

The strength of the computer science program. Factors to consider include the size and reputation of the program, the depth and variety of its curriculum, the professional standing of its faculty, whether any special programs or concentrations are offered, and its success in placing its students in interesting, rewarding positions when they graduate. Is the computer science department part of a College or School of Engineering? Is it accredited by ABET, the Accreditation Board for Engineering and Technology? At smaller colleges or universities, or schools without an engineering division, how adequate is the computer science curriculum? Will your coursework include computer architecture, data structures, language theory, and systems and hardware? Or does the curriculum consist primarily of courses in programming languages?

Computing facilities. Do the college and its computer science department offer a variety of computer equipment, from mainframes to microcomputers? How easy is it for students to gain access to these facilities to complete labs and homework assignments? Are there enough terminals to meet student demand? (Incidentally, some colleges and universities have begun to require or suggest that students bring their own microcomputer to campus as one of the necessary tools of higher education.)

The general strength and reputation of the college or university. This can be reflected in part by the general prestige of a school, its national and local reputation and the success of its alumni. You should also consider the breadth of a school's general curriculum (Will you receive a well-rounded education?), the faculty-student ratio, and the average SAT or ACT scores of its students.

Location, cost, and availability of student loans and other financial aid. The relative importance of these factors will vary for each individual.

The physical plant. What are the overall characteristics of dormitories, classroom buildings, and grounds? Is the campus attractive and well-maintained? Is security sufficient at urban campuses?

Other qualities. Many other, less specific qualities may enter into your choice of a college or university. Did your parents attend the school? A school's traditions, attitudes, and quality-of-life may influence your decision. Remember, however, that your first concern should be to select the school that will give you the best computer science education in the context of a good general education.

Many books are available that will help you to answer these questions and make an informed choice of a college or university. You may wish to consult one or more of the following:

> *American Universities and Colleges* (Washington, D.C.: American Council on Education).
> *Barron's Profiles of American Colleges* (Woodbury, NY: Barron's Educational Series).
> *The College Blue Book* (New York: Macmillan Publishing Company, Inc.).
> *The College Handbook* (published by the College Entrance Examination Board).
> *Comparative Guide to American Colleges* (New York: Harper and Row).
> *Lovejoy's College Guide* (New York: Monarch Press).
> *National College Databook* (Princeton, NJ: Peterson's Guides).
> *Peterson's Annual Guide to Undergraduate Study: Four-Year Colleges* (Princeton, NJ: Peterson's Guides).
> *Selective Guide to Colleges* (New York: Times Books).

Undergraduate Computer Science Curricula

The two largest organizations of computer professionals, the Association for Computing Machinery (ACM) and the IEEE Computer Society, have prepared model curricula for undergraduate degree programs in computer science. These curricula will give you some idea of what your undergraduate curriculum will include. They will also help you to evaluate the schools and programs you may consider. Examine these programs and compare them to the courses and degree plans at these schools. While there is much room for individual difference, if the program offered by a school deviates too greatly from these models, you should talk with a departmental representative to find out why, or perhaps consider another college or university.

*The ACM curriculum.** The ACM model curriculum is meant to be both general and flexible. It is the kind of program that might be found at a liberal arts or other four-year college that does not have a School of Engineering. It is built around a solid core of computer science courses. But it offers the student a good deal of flexibility to adapt it to his or her own special interests. A technical or business minor, or a minor in an unrelated discipline, is possible.

ACM recommends that computer science majors take at least 36 semester hours in computer science and 15 hours in mathematics, in addition to the requirements and electives identified by the individual college or university. All computer science majors take a series of eight core courses, plus four additional courses selected from a list of suggested electives. The core curriculum consists of the following eight courses:

Computer Programming I
Computer Programming II
Introduction to Computer Systems
Introduction to Computer Organization
Introduction to File Processing
Operating Systems and Computer Architecture I

---

*Curriculum '78, *"Communications of the ACM.* Vol. 22, No. 3 (March, 1979), pp. 147-166. Copyright 1979, Association for Computing Machinery, by permission.

Data Structures and Algorithm Analysis
Organization of Programming Languages
Students then elect to take four or more courses from the following:
Computers and Society
Operating Systems and Computer Architecture II
Database Management Systems Design
Artificial Intelligence
Algorithms
Software Development and Design
Theory of Programming Languages
Automata, Computability, and Formal Languages
Numerical Mathematics: Analysis
Numerical Mathematics: Linear Algebra

Computer science elective requirements can also be fulfilled by taking "special topics" courses such as microcomputer laboratory, telecommunications/networks/distributed systems, systems simulation, computer graphics, compiler writing, and simulation and modeling.

The ACM recommendations stress the importance of a solid background in mathematics for all computer science majors. Analytical and algebraic techniques, logic, finite mathematics, linear algebra, combinatorics, graph theory, optimization methods, and probability and statistics are all considered important additions to a student's curriculum. The following courses are recommended. These courses are taught in departments of mathematics or statistics:

Introductory Calculus
Mathematical Analysis I
Probability
Linear Algebra
Discrete Structures
Mathematical Analysis II
Probability and Statistics

The remainder of a student's curriculum may be largely dictated by the general course requirements of each school. The ACM report does make some suggestions, however. Notably, writing and communications skills are judged to be extremely important, especially because many employers look for these skills when reviewing job applicants.

Recommended science and engineering courses include, where available, electrical engineering courses such as digital logic and switching circuits; physics; and, because of an increasing emphasis on computing in these fields, courses in biological and environmental sciences.

For the many students who will work in business-oriented computing, ACM suggests coursework in business to obtain the background necessary to function productively in this area.

*The IEEE Computer Society Model Curriculum.** In December, 1983, the Educational Activities Board and Governing Board of the IEEE Computer Society approved the "1983 IEEE Computer Society Model Program in Computer Science and Engineering."

The Accreditation Board for Engineering and Technology (ABET), jointly sponsored by the major engineering professional societies, awards accreditation to engineering programs that meet ABET-defined requirements. Within ABET, the IEEE Computer Society is principally responsible for defining accreditation requirements for computer science and similarly-named programs. Thus, the IEEE Computer Society's proposed curriculum is designed to satisfy the minimum ABET requirements for any field of engineering. It is also meant to outline the criteria for an acceptable, high-caliber program in computer science or computer engineering.

The following four-year program represents, then, what you might follow if you enroll in a computer science program within a school of engineering. It is more engineering-oriented than the ACM program described above. If you are interested in the more technical aspects of computing, in computer science theory, or in working for major computer vendors in research and development, you should seek out an undergraduate program of this sort.

Two versions of the IEEE Computer Society model curriculum are given below, the first for a school on the semester system, the

---

*Copyright 1983, IEEE, by permission.

second for a school on the quarter or trimester system.

Semester system. The following is a semester-based program of 134 semester credit hours.

Freshman Year
First Semester

Department	Course	Credit Hours
Chem 101	Chemistry 1	4
Math 101	Calculus I	4
CSE 101	Introduction to Computing I	3
English 100	English Composition	3
	Humanities/Social Science Elective	3
	Total Hours	17

Second Semester

Physics 101	Physics I	4
Math 102	Calculus II	4
CSE 102	Introduction to Computing II	3
	Humanities/Social Science Electives	6
	Total Hours	17

Sophomore Year
First Semester

Physics 201	Physics II	4
Math 201	Calculus III	3
CSE 201	Introduction to Computer Engineering: Hardware & Software Design	3
CSE 202	Discrete Structures	3
	Humanities/Social Science Elective	3
	Total Hours	16

Second Semester

	Science Elective	4
Math 202	Differential Equations	4
CSE 203	Introductory Hardware Design Lab	3
EE 201	Basic Circuits & Electronics	3
	Humanities/Social Science Elective	3
	Total Hours	17

Junior Year
First Semester

CSE 301	Hardware System Design Lab	3
CSE 302	Software Engineering & Assembler Programming	4
EE 301	Linear Systems Analysis	3
STAT 301	Probability and Statistics	3
	Elective	3
	Total Hours	16

Second Semester

CSE 303	Software Engineering	3
ES 301	Engineering Science (Mechanics)	3
	Professional Electives (See Table 1)	6
	Elective	3
	Total Hours	15

Senior Year
First Semester

CSE 401	Design Lab	3
	Professional Electives	9 or 12
	Elective	3 or 6
	Total Hours	18

Second Semester

CSE 402	Design Lab	3
	Professional Electives	9 or 12
	Elective	3 or 6
	Total Hours	18

At a college or university on the quarter system, the curriculum for a B.S. in computer science or computer engineering should resemble the following model program.

Freshman Year
First Quarter

Department	**Course**	**Credit Hours**
Math 101	Calculus I	4
Engl 101	English I	3
Hist 101	History I	3
Phys 101	Physics I	4
CSE 101	Introduction to Computing I	3
	Total Hours	17

Second Quarter

Math 102	Calculus II	4
Engl 102	English II	3
Hist 102	History II	3
Phys 102	Physics II	4
CSE 102	Introduction to Computing II	3
	Total Hours	17

Third Quarter

Math 102	Calculus III	4
Engl 102	English III	3
Hist 103	History III	3
Phys 103	Physics III	4
CSE 103	Discrete Structures I	3
	Total Hours	17

Sophomore Year
First Quarter

Chem 201	Chemistry	4
Math 201	Calculus IV	5
Econ 201	Economics	5
CSE 201	Discrete Structures II	3
	Total Hours	17

Second Quarter

	Basic Science Elective	4
Math 202	Differential Equations	3
CSE 202	Logic Design	4
EE 201	Circuits I	3
CSE 203	Data Structures	4
	Total Hours	18

Third Quarter

Math 203	Linear Algebra	3
Phys 201	Modern Physics	3
CSE 204	Systems Programming	4
CSE 205	Digital Systems Design	5
	Total Hours	15

Junior Year
First Quarter

CSE 301	Computer Architecture	4
CSE 302	Digital Systems Lab	5
CSE 303	Software Lab	3
	Humanities/Social Science Elective	5
	Total Hours	17

Second Quarter

IE 301	Statistics	3
CSE 304	Computer Languages	4
CSE 305	Operating Systems	5
EE 301	Linear Systems	3
	Professional Elective	3
	Total Hours	18

Third Quarter

CSE 306	Interfacing	4
CSE 307	System Lab	4
Engl 301	Technical Writing	3
IE 302	Engineering Economics	3
	Professional Elective	3
	Total Hours	17

Senior Year
First Quarter

CSE 401	Design Project	3
	Professional Electives	13
	Total Hours	16

Second Quarter

CSE 402	Design Project	3
	Professional Electives	11
	Humanities/Social Science Elective	3
	Total Hours	17

Third Quarter

CSE 403	Design Project	3
	Professional Electives	11
	Humanities/Social Science Elective	3
	Total Hours	17

TABLE 1. PROFESSIONAL ELECTIVES CLASSED
ACCORDING TO AREAS OF CONCENTRATION

	Software Engineering	Computer System Design	Knowledge-Based Systems
Junior Year	Compilers and Translators	Architecture	Database Systems
	Intro to Performance Analysis	Advanced Electronics	Theory of Computing
Senior Year	Operating Systems	Computer Communication Networks	Operating Systems
	Database Systems	Operating Systems	Artificial Intelligence
	Theory of Computing	Compilers & Translators	Architecture
	Translator Writing Systems	Design Automation	Compilers and Translators
	Architecture	Intro to Performance Analysis	Computer Communication Networks
	Computer Communication Networks	VLSI System Design	Distributed Databases
	Design and Analysis of Algorithms	Fault-Tolerant Computing	Graphics

Note that these curricula are strongly engineering-oriented. Professional electives allow students the chance to take additional computer science courses as well as courses in electrical engineering, mathematics, or other technical subjects. Most other elective study would be devoted to satisfying the breadth requirements of the individual college or university. A student interested in business applications or management could conceivably use professional and any other available electives to take courses in accounting, finance, and management.

Some general remarks. The core of your undergraduate curriculum will consist of courses in computer science theory and applications. You can expect to be assigned many lab or homework problems that will require extensive time on the machines.

In addition to your classes in computer science, you will enroll in required and elective courses in mathematics, natural sciences, the humanities (and perhaps communication skills), and the social sciences. You will probably take at least a few courses in another engineering field or in business.

Mathematics is clearly an important field of study for computer scientists. Both the ACM and IEEE Computer Society emphasize mathematics study. The IEEE Computer Society proposed curriculum specifies that the following subjects should be covered by your mathematics coursework:

- Differential and Integral Calculus with Analytic Geometry
- Discrete Structures
- Applied Modern Algebra

For a program to be accredited by ABET, students must additionally complete at least one course in the following: differential equations, linear algebra, or numerical analysis.

Most colleges and universities have science requirements established for students in each major. In order to receive ABET accreditation, an engineering program must include four or five courses in general sciences. For the computer science student, physics is a clear choice. The fundamental laws of physics involved in electricity, electrostatics, electromagnetism, thermodynamics, mechanics, and even optics are central to understanding the principles of computer technology. In addition, you may want to consider courses in biology or biomedical sciences if you are interested in the medical applications of computer science, or in human factors research. (Human factors studies the man-machine interface: that is, the way humans relate physically and psychologically to machines.) Physiology courses are also helpful in human factors study and in robotics and problems in human-machine information processing.

The humanities include history, philosophy, literature, and the fine arts. Most colleges and universities require that you complete a number of humanities courses to ensure that their graduates are well-rounded, literate individuals. As a student in computer science, you may find courses in the humanities (and the social sciences) a refreshing change from your technical studies. Learning to appreciate art or literature or music and becoming informed about the history of human culture will enrich you in ways you will appreciate for the rest of your life.

Like the ACM curriculum, the IEEE Computer Society recommends that computer science students take courses in writing and communications skills. Courses in technical writing, technical editing, and advanced composition (emphasizing practical rather than literary writing) will help you document your programs better. And your specialized knowledge of computer science will be of little value if you cannot communicate it in an understandable way to those who need your expertise. Students interested in programming language theory, natural language processing, and artificial intelligence will find courses in linguistics useful.

In business applications, management, and marketing and sales, oral communication skills are essential. Courses in speech communication, including technical or professional speaking and group or organizational communication, will help you to develop these skills. And a better understanding of human communication strategies will enable even the most technically-minded individual to work more productively as a member of a project team.

The social sciences include anthropology, psychology, sociology, political science, and economics. Most colleges require some coursework in these subjects. Psychology, especially cognitive psychology, will be useful to students interested in artificial intelligence, pattern recognition, or human factors. Learning how the human brain can perceive and think can lead to better modeling of thought in machine applications.

For students interested in business applications, economics courses are important. Study of economics will help you to understand the fundamental principles underlying modern business and financial transactions and decision-making. Political science will give you a better comprehension of ways in which economic and political structures are affected by computer technology. It is clearly important for those of you who will be responsible for advances in technology to understand the implications and consequences of these advances. And a better understanding of political and economic forces will make you a better citizen of your country and of the global community.

In selecting engineering courses, choose courses that will be of service to you in the context of your career goals. If you are interested in hardware, coursework in electronics, instrumentation, or control theory will supplement your work in electrical engineering. If you are interested in computer-aided manufacture and robotics, courses in advanced mechanics and industrial engineering are appropriate. A good advisor in your computer science department can help you to select these courses wisely.

For those interested in business applications, systems analysis, or information management, study of accounting, finance, and management is important. You should also consider the option of enrolling in a degree program especially designed for business-related computing applications. These programs are variously called information science, systems science, or data processing. Other degree programs emphasizing a range of computer applications in business and industry include systems analysis, systems engineering, industrial engineering, management science, and operations research. Most of these programs place less emphasis on the theoretical and engineering aspects of computers and more emphasis on practical problems of providing automated systems to do the work of business and industry.

Financial Aid

A four-year college education is an expensive investment. In 1983, it was estimated that residential students paid on average $4,700 to attend a four-year publicly-funded institution. The average for private colleges and universities was around $8,440. Private schools in New England averaged over $10,000, with some renowned institutions ranging several thousand dollars above that figure. And costs for commuter students were not significantly lower, averaging $3,800 at state colleges and universities and $7,300 at private schools.

In addition to basic tuition and fees, you will need to pay for room, board, books, supplies, and incidental expenses. These costs mount up rapidly. Moreover, the cost of higher education has increased annually for several years now.

There is no doubt that obtaining a college education is worth this expense. Not only is a college degree a ticket to higher paying and more responsible jobs in many fields. A college education gives you a rich foundation in cultural and historical knowledge that will enhance the quality of your life.

For many students, then, the question is, How to finance that education? Many sources of financial assistance are available to help defray the cost of your college education. It is important, however, to plan ahead if you are seeking financial assistance. Begin at least a year before you expect to start college.

Types of financial aid include: 1) grants and loans based on a student's simple need; 2) grants and loans based on a student's (or a student's family's) ability to pay; 3) work-study programs; and 4) scholarships, grants, and awards made in recognition of a student's accomplishments or academic potential. Sources of financial aid include federal and state governments, foundations, civic groups, fraternal organizations, professional organizations, individual colleges and universities, and major corporations.

Some forms of federally-backed financial aid include:

- Pell Grants. Established in 1980 under the new Higher Education Ammendments Act, Pell Grants are based on your family's need. In 1983-84, these grants ranged as high as $1,800.

- Guaranteed Student Loan Program. The Guaranteed Student Loan program supports loans to students made by local banks and savings and loan associations at attractive interest rates. You do not begin repaying these loans until some months after you graduate.
- Supplemental Educational Opportunity Grant Program. This program awards grants of up to $2,000 a year. Awards are based on a student's financial need.
- National Direct Student Loan Program. Loans administered under this program are awarded by college financial aid offices. These low-interest loans are repaid to your college after your graduation.
- College Work-Study Program. This campus-based program enables students to work a certain number of hours each week to earn part of their college expenses.

Many other kinds of financial aid are available. The following are a few of the many books on this subject:

Barron's Guide to Scholarships and Financial Aid (Woodbury, NY: Barron's Educational Series).

The College Money Handbook (Princeton, NJ: Peterson's Guides).

Dollars for Scholars Student Aid Catalogs. This is a series of state-by-state guides to financial aid. (Princeton, NJ: Peterson's Guides).

Financing College Education (New York: Harper Colophon Books).

Lovejoy's Guide to Scholarships and Grants (New York: Monarch Press).

Part-Time and Summer Employment

Many students help pay for the cost of their education by taking part-time jobs during academic terms or full- or part-time jobs during summers.

It is difficult to work more than a few hours a week and still have the time and energy to give your best efforts to your studies. And as we have seen, undergraduate programs in computer science are extremely demanding. Furthermore, at some colleges, students' access to computing equipment may be limited to certain hours, for instance, in the evenings and on weekends when the system is not being used for administrative and research purposes. Thus, many computer science students will find it hard to work during school terms. To do so and still do well in school takes self-discipline and, sometimes, an understanding, flexible employer. In considering working during school, be realistic in assessing your determination and your schedule. If you need or want to work while attending classes, make sure you are willing to sacrifice what little leisure time your studies may allow.

One kind of work, though, needs no word of caution. Any computer-related work experience you gain during school terms and summers will be useful to you. The wise computer student will seek out jobs in the machine room or at the help desk. Such experience will increase the meaningfulness and relevance of your coursework. Moreover, employers seek out graduates with computer-related work experience in entry-level hiring. As we have seen, computer professionals are unanimous in stressing the benefits of this experience. Work in computer operations is considered an excellent complement to the abstract or programming emphasis of many degree programs in computer science.

Summer vacations provide a good opportunity to obtain work experience and earn money to pay for college expenses. One way to find summer work is to talk to the computing center on your campus and to professors responsible for smaller computer labs. You can also contact local employers: even a summer as a data entry clerk will give you valuable experience and a paycheck.

Summer Work and Intern or Cooperative Programs in Industry

Working in the computer industry during summers or as part of a cooperative education or internship program can give you valuable experience. You will gain a first-hand knowledge of the real-world work environment. And you will greatly expand your knowledge of computers and computing. Furthermore, many students who do well as interns or co-op workers receive offers of employment when they graduate.

Peterson's Guide to Engineering, Science, and Computer Jobs lists larger companies that hire students for summer work. You can also approach local employers of computer personnel. Your college placement office can often be of assistance. Your departmental advisor may know of summer work opportunities, as well as being able to tell you about intern and cooperative programs.

GRADUATE STUDY

As growing numbers of students graduate with a B.S. in Computer Science, competition for entry-level jobs has increased. For many individuals, graduate school will be an attractive option.

There are a number of reasons why you may wish to seek an advanced degree. Many positions in research and development require at least a Master's degree, and in some cases, as we have seen, a Ph.D.. Individuals aiming for management positions will find that an M.B.A. (Master of Business Administration), combined with an undergraduate computer science degree, will make them very attractive to employers. And a graduate degree in computer science, usually at the Master's level, affords those with undergraduate degrees in other disciplines to gain entry into the computer field. Finally, the Ph.D. is generally necessary to teach computer science at the college level.

The Master's Degree in Computer Science

The Master's degree requires a minimum of 32 to 36 semester credit hours of study beyond the bachelor's degree. Some programs require completion of a thesis; others offer thesis and non-thesis options. You will, however, probably have to complete some kind of original research or programming project. You will certainly have to pass a comprehensive oral or written exam.

Two groups of people will benefit from taking a master's in computer science. First, if you wish to specialize in a certain area, such as computer architecture or software engineering, but are not ready or willing to commit yourself to a lengthy doctoral program, graduate study at the Master's level may be your answer. If you are considering working towards a Ph.D., but want to test your aptitude and interest in graduate-level study, a Master's program gives you this opportunity. After a year, you can leave academic study and take a job in industry. Or you can continue toward your doctorate.

A second group finds that the Master's degree gives necessary proof of qualifications for employment in the computer field. These are people whose undergraduate degree is in another discipline, often the liberal arts or social sciences. For these individuals, a good way to change the direction of their career is to obtain a Master's in computer science.

If you are coming into the computer field from another discipline, most computer science departments will ask you to successfully complete a number of undergraduate courses before admitting you to their master's program. This is necessary to give you the basic knowledge upon which your graduate courses will build. And it demonstrates to the department your ability to undertake more advanced study.

Before making a career change, it is best to enroll in one or two computer courses first. If you do well and, more importantly, if you enjoy computing, then make plans to study for your master's. But if you find you have to force yourself to program and to study, computer science is not for you. Find out first, before you make significant changes in your career goals.

The Ph.D. in Computer Science

The Ph.D. requires more than 90 semester hours of study beyond the bachelor's level and completion of a dissertation. It takes at least three years, often longer, to obtain a doctorate. Doctoral study allows you to do original research in computer science and qualifies you to teach in colleges and universities and to perform advanced research in industrial settings or research institutions.

The Association for Computing Machinery annually publishes a *Graduate Assistantship Directory* listing grants, fellowships, and assistantships available in computer science departments throughout the U.S. ACM also presents the Doctoral Dissertation Award for the outstanding dissertation in computer science and engineering entered in open competition.

CERTIFICATION

Many professions, such as law, medicine, or accounting, have certification procedures to insure that their members are competent. There are no industry-wide certification standards for computer professionals. However, the Institute for Certification of Computer Professionals (35 East Wacker Drive, Chicago, IL 60601) awards two certificates: the Certificate in Data Processing and the Certificate in Computer Programming. The ICCP is a non-profit organization established for the purpose of testing and certifying the knowledge and skills of computer professionals. Its charter members include most of the major professional organizations in the computer and data processing field. Certificates are awarded on the basis of tests administered annually at selected college and university sites throughout the U.S. and Canada and overseas.

COMPANY-SPONSORED EDUCATION AND TRAINING

Your education in computer science does not end when you receive your college degree. In many ways, it is just beginning. For the first six to eight months you are on the job, you will be learning about company equipment, software, and procedures. This training may be formal or informal. How well you do during this initial period can affect your future success, as many employers see this as a probationary period.

Because of the rapid rate of technological change in the computer field, most larger companies offer many opportunities for the continuing education of their employees. Many sponsor both internal and external educational programs.

Internal training programs, designed to keep employees up-to-date with current technological advances, range from general development courses to short-term seminars on specific technical issues. These courses are usually supervised and staffed by the company educational services division.

Many employers encourage their workers to go outside the company to further their education. For instance, many sponsor employee enrollment in M.B.A. programs to prepare technically-knowledgeable people to move into management. An especially valuable benefit to you as an employee will be your company's tuition reimbursement program. In these programs, the employer will cover the costs—tuition, fees, and books—as you work on an additional undergraduate or graduate degree. Any undergraduate seriously considering attending graduate school will do well to consider employment with an organization offering tuition reimbursement.

Some companies offer classes at their facilities taught by faculty from nearby colleges and universities. These courses may be general in nature, designed to improve employee productivity and professionalism. Subjects like public speaking and technical writing are popular. Some large computer vendors may even offer full undergraduate and graduate programs at their facilities in selected subjects such as electrical engineering and computer science.

Companies that invest in employee education consider their money well-spent. Their investment pays off in better-educated, more up-to-date employees, informed about advances in the computer field and better able to perform their jobs. A technologically-obsolete employee is of little worth in a field as dynamic as computer science.

Asking intelligent questions at the job interview can save everyone time and misunderstandings. Photo: Bell & Howell Education Group.

CHAPTER 7

FINDING YOUR FIRST JOB

Until fairly recently, anyone who could write a COBOL program could get a job. If you held an undergraduate degree in computer science, you could pick and choose among several offers of employment. Each year, however, more and more students graduate with four-year degrees in computer-related subjects. And each year, the competition for entry-level positions grows increasingly stiff.

What can you do to guarantee that you leave school with a promise of employment? How do you go about finding a satisfying job? What questions should you ask before you accept employment? And how do you choose wisely among more than one job offer? These and related questions will be discussed in this chapter.

INFORMATION ABOUT EMPLOYERS

There are a number of ways to find out about potential employers and to bring your qualifications to their attention. Vacancies are advertised in newspapers and trade journals, and some general employment guides are published each year. You can write directly to a company inquiring about openings. And you can use personal contacts to get a foot in the door. Very likely, you may find your first job through campus recruiting efforts on the part of large employers.

In seeking a position in the computer field, your first stop should be the immensely helpful *Peterson's Guide to Engineering, Science, and Computer Jobs.* Published annually, *Peterson's* lists employers who are hiring computer science graduates for positions in research and development, production, technical services, information systems and information processing, marketing and sales, and administration and finance. Each employer is briefly described, together with basic information on hiring needs, starting salaries, and the ratio of applicants to job offers. The name and address of the individual you should contact concerning employment is also provided.

You may also want to look at the *College Placement Annual,* an occupational directory listing information on positions in all fields customarily offered to college graduates.

Many computer science and information processing positions are advertised in trade publications like *Computerworld,* and in the classified section of major metropolitan newspapers. Most of the positions listed will be for experienced personnel. Do not be overly discouraged by this. Many companies that regularly hire recent graduates to not advertise entry-level positions. If you do find yourself qualified for an advertised position, remember that you must respond promptly. The earlier your letter of application and resume are received, the better chance you will have to be actively considered for the job.

Most entry-level positions in the computer field are not found through classified or trade journal advertisements, however. What other avenues are open to you? How should you go about finding your first job?

Because of the current demand for computer science graduates, you may find yourself in an unusual position: you may find that an employer is asking you to apply for a job. Large employers of computer specialists sometimes obtain a list of graduating students from computer science departments or schools of engineering. You may receive a letter from such an employer (or recruiter: the U.S. military sometimes uses this approach). By all means, apply for such a job if it is of interest to you. But do not expect too much. Companies who send out blanket invitations for applications are looking for very specific qualifications. It may be purely a matter of chance if your background exactly fits their staffing needs. Pursue other possibilities.

You can contact an employer directly. You can submit a letter of application, together with your resume, outlining your qualifications and interests, to a prospective employer. You might also, if it is convenient, visit a company and talk with someone about the kinds of work done at that facility. Many companies will gladly talk to interested individuals about their work. Sometimes, such informal contact can lead to later employment.

Your computer science professors may also be able to assist you to find a suitable position. Many professors maintain contacts with industry; some work in industry as consultants. These individuals are often willing to aid students who they know to be well-trained, hard-working, and professionally motivated.

Your participation in student chapters of professional organizations such as the IEEE Computer Society, the Association for Computing Machinery, or the Data Processing Management Association, may also help you in your search for employment. These organizations frequently sponsor guest speakers from business, industry, and the academic world. Not only will their presentations inform you of timely or significant subjects in the field of computer science. Guest speakers will usually meet informally with interested students before or after their presentation. The motivated student can make useful industry contacts, learn of openings in the speaker's organization, or learn about other companies that may be hiring computer personnel.

Campus Recruitment

Many large companies send recruiters to colleges and universities with large or outstanding programs in computer science. In fact, in the computer industry many larger corporations may rely almost exclusively on campus recruitment to meet their entry-level staffing needs. For instance, in each of the years 1980 to 1983, IBM hired approximately 4,500 new employees through its extensive campus recruitment effort.

The campus recruiter will visit with qualified students interested in working for his or her company. These interviews are arranged through the school's career guidance and placement office, which will ordinarily post or publish a list of companies scheduled to conduct on-campus interviews and will set up individual appointments. If you plan to go through the campus recruitment process, plan ahead. You may have to sign up for interviews several weeks before the actual interview date.

The campus recruitment process allows companies to review a large number of job candidates quickly and easily. The on-campus interview gives the student a chance to learn about the company, its work, and its policies. Campus interviews also give you an opportunity to practice your interviewing techniques.

On-campus interviews are basically screening interviews. Few, if any, job offers will be made. More likely, successful candidates will be invited, at company expense, to visit company facilities. During this "plant trip," you will spend a day talking to a range of company personnel and will learn first-hand what it would be like to work for that organization.

Job Placement Services

Job placement services provide another way for employers and potential employees to establish contact with one another. Because computer science personnel are currently in high demand, the fee for such placement services is almost always paid by the employer. Some of these services (as well as some professional organizations) maintain and use computerized data bases to match employer needs with qualified applicants. These data bases make it possible for job candidates to limit their job search to a specific geographical location or kind of position. For instance, if you would like to work in systems programming in Minnesota or Texas, but do not wish to move to New York or Chicago, your electronic résumé will be routed only to employers in the regions you have specified.

Two of the placement services that specialize in finding jobs for computer professionals are Source EDP and Scientific Placement, Inc. Source EDP is a professional recruiting firm devoted exclusively to the computing field, with over 65 regional branch offices located in cities throughout the U.S. and Canada. Source EDP's professional staff is made up of people who have worked extensively in computing. Their own job experience enables them to provide informed counseling, career planning, and placement services to other computer professionals.

Scientific Placement, Inc. (P.O. Box 19949, Houston, TX, 77224) is a technical specialist placement firm focusing on high technology industries. It uses an on-line data base of job openings and résumés to find positions for technical professionals with undergraduate degrees in engineering, science, or computer science. Although Scientific Placement's offices are in Texas, it routinely places job candidates in cities throughout the U.S. and even overseas.

Technical Job Fairs

Technical job fairs bring together in one place many different companies seeking to hire qualified people trained in computer science and other technical and engineering disciplines. Job fairs are usually held at a hotel or other central location in large cities or in connection with major industry conventions, such as the National Computer Conference. These events will be well-publicized in newspapers and on radio.

At job fairs, employers set up information displays and company representatives will talk informally with interested individuals about their company and its work. Because of the demand in recent years for computer and engineering personnel, these job fairs have become a very popular way for employers and potential employees to find out about each other. While most companies at job fairs are looking for individuals with some work experience, students and recent graduates can still benefit from the opportunity to learn more directly about the computer industry and to meet people who may be of assistance in securing a first job.

JOB APPLICATION LETTERS AND RÉSUMÉS

If you are applying for an advertised position or inquiring about employment opportunities with a company, you will need to write a letter of application.

The job application letter is a three-to-four-paragraph summary of your education and qualifications for employment. It is accompanied by and introduces your résumé, which describes your credentials in considerably more detail.

In the first paragraph of your letter, you should identify the position you are seeking (be specific here) and how you found out about the opening, if it is relevant. You should also add a brief statement of your qualifications for the job.

In the second (and if necessary, third) paragraph of your letter, you describe your education, extracurricular activities, previous work experience, and any special skills or qualifications you may possess. Emphasize the way in which your education and experience increase your potential value to the organization to whom you are applying. (You may need to do some homework to find out about that organization to make this information convincing.) Remember, too, that concrete examples and details are much more effective than vague generalizations. "My summer and part-time work experience as an operator in my college's Computing Center has made me familiar with the day-to-day operations of a large data processing department" is much better than "I gained experience working summers."

The closing paragraph of your letter should indicate your willingness to be interviewed. If possible, suggest a specific period of time when you will be available, or let the company know when and how they can most easily reach you to make an appointment. And if you have not mentioned it earlier, this is the place to invite the reader to examine your enclosed résumé.

Throughout your letter of application, maintain a confident and professional tone. While all job letters are, in the final analysis, "sales pitches," avoid a bragging or aggressive tone. At the same time, realize that your degree in computer science is a substantial accomplishment of which you should be reasonably proud. Avoid humble or effusive language.

You can generally allow two to three weeks' response time from the date the company can be expected to have received your job letter and résumé. After that time, a follow-up letter or telephone call is not inappropriate.

Résumés

A résumé is a brief description of your education, experience, abilities, interests, and other information of concern to an employer. Résumés are of two sorts. A *descriptive* résumé lists, in reverse chronological order, your education and work experience. Descriptive résumés focus on what you have done in the past. A *functional* résumé (sometimes called a *qualifications brief*) emphasizes what you are able to do: your talents, skills, and abilities. Most résumés combine descriptive and functional features.

What information should you include in a résumé? Most good résumés will include the following:

- *Your name, address, and phone number.* This information should be placed conspicuously at the top of the page and can serve as a heading. There is no need to include the word, "resume," as this will be obvious to the reader. If you are still in school but are nearing graduation (or if for other reasons you include two addresses), make it clear to the reader to which address he or she should respond. You can label one "School Address," the other "Permanent Address," or specify "Address Until (date)" and "Address After (date)."

- *Career Objective.* In this section, you describe the type of position you are seeking. Be specific: "A position as an applications programmer that uses my knowledge of accounting" is far more effective than "Seeking an entry-level position in computing."

  The objective section may be omitted, but if well-written and precise, its inclusion projects an image of a knowledgeable professional. Sometimes, especially in the case of graduate students, this section is titled "Interests" and describes areas in which the job candidate wishes to concentrate.

- *Education.* Your degree (or degrees, if you have attended graduate school), major, college or university, and date of graduation are listed in this section, together with information on your minor or field of specialization. Other information may also be included. You may (and sometimes should) include a list of courses you have taken that are related to the position for which you are applying. If your grade point average is 3.0 or better, include this fact, as well as any honors, achievements, or awards. And if you have paid for part or all of your education, say so: companies are impressed with job applicants who demonstrate such responsibility and motivation. Sometimes extracurricular activities will be included in this section, sometimes placed under a separate heading.

- *Work Experience.* List the company, location, dates, and position of any work experience. Stress your responsibilities, the skills each job demanded, and the qualifications you gained from working. If you have held a number of diverse summer and part-time jobs, do not list every one. Describe them under a single, general heading. Highlight any work experience directly relevant to your career objective.

- *Computer Languages and Equipment Experience.* Most employers will want to know the programming languages you have used and the equipment and systems with which you are familiar. In describing the machines, give model, manufacturer, and operating system. Make lesser-known languages and equipment seem more familiar by describing them in terms of more widely-known examples.

- *Professional Affiliations and Activities.* Your membership in professional organizations testifies to your commitment to computers and computing. (See Chapter Nine for a list of some of these organizations.) List those organizations to which you belong and any other relevant professional activities. Sometimes, especially if you have been active in a student chapter of a professional group, you can combine this section with a description of your other extracurricular activities.

- *Other Facts.* While it is certainly true that your computer science degree and work experience will go a long way toward securing your employment, the more your resume reflects a well-rounded, interesting individual, the more arresting it will be. Sometimes this category is called "Personal" or "Personal Facts," or simply "Other." It may include, variously, your date (and place) of birth; your hobbies, interests, or special or unique qualifications. Do you have a pilot's license? Do you like to travel, ski, or garden? Do you speak a foreign language or have you lived abroad? These and other facts can be listed here. Married males will usually mention their marital status; others will not. You can also use this section to specify your geographical preference and willingness to relocate or travel. Information on your citizenship, military experience, and security clearances should also be provided. Many projects in the computer and other high technology industries are funded, directly or indirectly, by the U.S. Government. Individuals engaged in these projects may be required to hold U.S. citizenship.

- *References.* At the bottom of your résumé, you can indicate your willingness to supply references that will attest to your professional and personal qualifications. It is usually best to simply say that "References will be provided on request," instead of listing the names of your referees. This allows you some flexibility, too. You can supply names of different people to different employers. (Some employment experts feel the "References" section need not be included on a resume. Obviously, you will be expected to provide references if asked.)

You need to line up individuals willing to write recommendations for you well in advance of your job search. Professors and previous employers will be your best sources of professional references. Personal or character references can be provided by anyone who has known you well and can speak for your integrity and other character traits. Family friends, physicians, or religious leaders are likely choices. It is not a good idea, though, to ask fellow students for such references. Choose individuals whose opinion will have some weight and credibility with employers.

Always ask an individual if he or she feels able to recommend you. If someone feels able to provide only a lukewarm or very general recommendation, it is better to look elsewhere. When someone does agree to recommend you, give him or her a copy of your résumé. Sit down and talk with him or her about your background and career goals. The more referees know about your work and your ambitions, the more effective their recommendation will be.

Two model résumés are reproduced below. Both show the qualifications of recent graduates of the same computer science undergraduate program seeking employment in computing. The first shows an individual with a technical emphasis, the second someone with business skills and an interest in applications programming.

R. H. Sturtevant
333 Inverness Drive
Waco, Texas 76710
(817) 555-5555

OBJECTIVE:	Seeking a challenging position as a SYSTEMS PROGRAMMER/ANALYST in the computer or telecommunications industry.
EDUCATION:	B.S., Computer Science, Texas A&M University, College Station, Texas, May, 1984. Minor field of study in Industrial Engineering. GPA: 3.2. GPA in major: 3.5.
	Programming Projects: A trace program written in OS ALP and a control program linking several Texas Instruments microcomputers to form a pseudo-minicomputer.
PROGRAMMING LANGUAGES:	Assembly (ALP), FORTRAN, PL/1, C, Pascal, SNOBOL, APL, COBOL, and BASIC.

EQUIPMENT
EXPERIENCE:

AMDAHL 470 V6 and V7B with IBM MVS/JES3 Operating System; DATA GENERAL MV8000 with AOS/VS Operating System; Apple IIE; Texas Instruments Professional Microcomputer.

WORK
EXPERIENCE:

KWTX-TV, Waco, Texas. Worked as Program Director, On-Air Director, and Floor Director. Responsibilities included running commercials and other television network "cut-ins," organizing local television productions, supervising technical staff. Able to work successfully under tight time schedules. Employed 1977-1980.

KBTX-TV, Bryan, Texas. Worked part-time while in college to partially defray educational expenses. Duties essentially identical to those performed at KWTX. Employed 1981-83.

OTHER
FACTS:

Member, IEEE Computer Society, Association for Computing Machinery. Active in student chapters in ACM. Enjoy flying, backpacking, snow skiing, racquetball, and classical music. Prefer position in Texas or the Southwest.

REFERENCES:

Available on request from Placement Center, J. Earl Rudder Conference Tower, Texas A&M University, College Station, Texas 77843.

Jeffrey A. Jekel
P.O. Box 99999
College Station, Texas 77844
(409) 555-5555

objective

Seeking a position as an applications programmer/ analyst that uses my accounting skills in a business data processing environment.

education

B.S., Computer Science, Texas A&M University, College Station, Texas, May, 1984. Successfully completed eighteen hours of Accounting. Maintained a 3.43 grade point average in major field of study. Earned 25% of educational expenses.

programming languages	Programming coursework emphasized structured programming techniques. Languages include IBM 360/370 Assembler, COBOL, PL/1, PASCAL, BASIC, APL.
equipment experience	Amdahl 470 V6 and V7B with IBM MVS/JES3 Input Service; Data General MV800 with AOS/VS Operating System; Apple, Radio Shack, and Texas Instruments microcomputers.
professional affiliations & extracurricular activities	Member of Association for Computing Machinery, IEEE Computer Society, and Data Processing Management Association. Participated in intramural sports: volleyball, racquetball, squash.
work experience, 1980-83	Worked during summers and holidays for Pizza Hut, Incorporated, in Kingsville, Texas. Promoted to shift leader and given responsibility for all aspects of restaurant operations in manager's absence.
other information	Born September, 1961, San Antonio, Texas. Married. Interests include beekeeping, organic gardening, reading, travel. Willing to relocate and to retrain to meet company needs.
references	References furnished on request.

PREPARING FOR AN INTERVIEW

It is extremely important to prepare for a job interview by finding out as much as possible about the company with whom you will be talking. A trip to the library can help. You might begin by looking up the company in *Standard and Poor's Register of Corporation Executives* or *Dun and Bradstreet's Million Dollar Directory*. These two publications give general information about larger American corporations. If the company is publicly traded, more specialized information can be found in the quarterly and annual reports to stockholders. These reports may be available in your campus library or can be obtained by writing directly to the company. Some knowledge of a company's financial situation will be especially important to job candidates emphasizing business applications of computers.

Newspaper and magazine articles give the most recent information about how and what a company is doing and are good for finding out about technical developments as well as company problems. A simple way to find out what has been published about a company is to look it up in *Business Periodicals Index,* the *F&S Index,* or the *Index* to the *Wall Street Journal.*

Reading popular publications like *Computerworld* and *Datamation* can keep you up to date on overall trends and advances in the computer industry. Most large corporations prepare their own recruiting literature to inform applicants about their work. These publications may be on file in your college placement office.

What kinds of questions can you expect an interviewer to ask? Most interviewers will want to know about your academic background: which courses you enjoyed, which you did not like, and how your education prepares you for the opportunities their organization offers. They will ask you about your extracurricular activities, interests, and work experience. You may be asked to identify your strengths and accomplishments—and your weaknesses. Interviewers look for candidates with clear career goals. The more you know about the kind of work you want to do in the computer field, the better you will be able to respond to questions about your career direction. And many interviewers will want to know where, based on what you know about their operations, you see yourself most effectively working. Again, note that the best-prepared job candidate has done his or her homework on the company.

Some other general guidelines to help you interview successfully include:

- Be punctual. Be on time—or better, arrive a few minutes early so you can gather your thoughts and catch your breath before the interview begins.
- Dress professionally. Whether you like it or not, visual impressions are important. And here, IBM has set the industry standard: dark suit, white or neutral shirt or blouse, the

dress-for-success image. While you may find that in some computer companies, jeans and hiking boots are the standard attire, wait until you have a job to adopt less conservative dress. Even then, strive to project an image of professionalism.

- Be personable. Maintain good eye contact, shake hands firmly, smile. Be positive, confident, poised, enthusiastic. Listen actively to the interviewer's questions. A successful interview is a dialogue, not an interrogation.

- Ask questions. The interview is your chance to learn about the employment and advancement opportunities, working conditions, special programs, benefits, and general atmosphere in which you will be working. Your research will help you prepare specific questions for the interviewer. Asking informed questions will also demonstrate your interest in the company.

Be sure to obtain the interviewer's name, title, and company address. Within a day or two of your interview, write a short follow-up letter, thanking the interviewer for taking time to talk to you about the company. You might point out a feature of working with that company that particularly interests you, and express your continuing interest in employment.

Most interviewers will tell you when you can expect to hear from them. If they do not, be sure to ask them for a date. You can do this gracefully by pointing out that you are interviewing with other companies and would like to know when you can expect their decision to be made.

In general, approach the interview and your overall search for employment with two thoughts in mind:

- Employers hire *people*, not degrees.
- Employers hire people to do *something*, not anything. Set clear career objectives.

SOME PRACTICAL SUGGESTIONS

Experienced job hunters know that the search for employment can itself become a nearly full-time job. And finding a job takes research skills, organization, and persistence, even in the computer field where so many opportunities exist. Plan to devote a considerable amount of time and energy to your job search. If you are still in school, you may want to plan your last semester so that you have enough time to look for employment without sacrificing your academic standing.

Some very practical suggestions:
- Buy yourself a calendar. Write down appointments, interviews, and dates you can expect to hear from employers. Also record all telephone conversations and the dates you send out letters and résumés.
- Keep copies of all correspondence with employers. You may need to refer to this correspondence.
- Be persistent and follow through on all leads. If you send out a job letter and do not receive a response within two to three weeks, write or telephone the employer to inquire about your status. If an interviewer says that you will hear from them in three weeks and you do not, make a phone call. Your papers may have been lost in the shuffle.
- Do not take rejection personally. Your qualifications will not suit the hiring needs of all employers. This does not make you any less qualified.

EVALUATING EMPLOYMENT OFFERS

When you receive an offer of employment, there are a number of factors you should consider before accepting the job, especially if you are trying to choose among more than one offer. Some things to think about include:
- *Benefits.* It may seem strange to be thinking about retire-

ment when you have not yet started your first job. But retirement, life, health, and dental insurance, disability coverage, and investment plans are no less a part of your total salary than is your basic wage. You may find it difficult to read through the description of employee benefits, which may be written in opaque and legalistic language. Try, however, to make a list of benefits provided by the employer and calculate their worth. In comparing two employers, one offering a higher salary, the other better benefits, subtract the value of those benefits from the more attractive salary to see what you really will be making.

- *Geographical location.* The cost of living in different parts of the country varies dramatically. What is a high salary in Baltimore or Atlanta may not go very far in Los Angeles or New York. You must decide how important living in a particular city, state, or region is to you. You may need to accommodate your geographical preferences to the realities of the job market. Are you more concerned with what you do or where you do it?

- *Opportunities for advancement.* Will a position allow you to grow and develop professionally? What chance will you have to move upward and outward in the organization? Will working for this employer help you to achieve your career goals? What is the employer's policy regarding promotions?

- *Employment security.* A young, expanding company may offer opportunities for rapid advancement. At the same time, it may be financially less stable. Do you seek the security of an established company or are you attracted by the advantages and risks of a more volatile organization?

- *Company style.* Some companies are conservative in appearance, attitude, and procedures. Some foster competitive, fast-paced, intense working conditions. Others are more measured, relaxed, or stratified. Try to match your own characteristics to the style of an organization. Select the employer with whom you will feel most comfortable. That employer will be most comfortable with you.

CHAPTER 8

EMPLOYMENT OUTLOOK

Computer science and information processing personnel are among the most sought after and better paid professionals. It is easy to imagine that a computer science degree will guarantee a good job and an attractive salary. It is easy to presume that the demand for computer scientists will be unlimited in coming years. In fact, government figures predict that by 1995, only one job in fifteen will be in high technology. While within the computer field, demand is expected to roughly double, much greater rates of employment growth will be in menial service positions.

In this chapter, we will look at the geographical distribution of professional employment in the computer field. We will also examine trends in demand, opportunities for advancement, and directions of future growth in the computer industry.

GEOGRAPHICAL DISTRIBUTION

At the end of the 1970's most computer-related employment was concentrated in major metropolitan areas where companies using large, general-purpose mainframe computers were located. And even today, a large number of positions are located in major cities. New York, Los Angeles, San Francisco, and Dallas-Ft. Worth have large concentrations of computer professionals. The route from Washington, DC, to Frederick, Maryland, has become an increasingly important center of employment because of its proximity to federal government agencies. And while most computer vendors have facilities in many regions of the country, vendor activity remains strongest in three states: California, Massachusetts, and Texas. Much of the work in research and product development takes place in California's famed "Silicon Valley" and along Massachusetts' Highway 30 out of Boston. And Texas, especially the "Silicon Gulch" surrounding Austin, is becoming an important center of research, development, and manufacturing. This growth was bolstered by the decision, in 1983, to locate the Microelectronics and Computer Technology Corporation in Austin. (MCC is an influential consortium of major computer companies dedicated to insuring American preeminance in the computer field.)

Jobs in computing are not, as we have seen, by any means limited to computer vendors. In information and data processing, and in business applications, opportunities exist throughout the U.S. in banking, insurance, education, manufacturing, and government: in short, in any industry needing to process large quantities of information. Again, though, a significant number of these positions will be clustered in urban and suburban areas.

Increased use of microcomputers and advances in telecommunications are decentralizing computer work. In the future, workers in many fields may work at home or in regional facilities at some distance from their employers. Already, some professionals work from their home computer terminal one or two days a week, commuting to the office on remaining days. Although at present these opportunities are rare, they represent a growing trend toward widely distributed employment patterns.

DEMAND

Steady growth in the demand for qualified computer professionals shows every indication of continuing throughout the 1980's and beyond. Widely reported figures prepared by the U.S. Bureau of Labor Statistics indicate that total employment of computer-related personnel is expected to grow 47.1 percent between 1980 and 1990, from 1,455,000 to 2,140,000. This estimate includes computer support personnel as well as programmers and systems analysts. During this same period, employment of programmers is expected to grow at almost the same rate as overall computer-related employment: 46.6 percent, or from 341,000 to 500,000. The demand for systems analysts is expected to grow at an even greater rate: from 243,000 in 1980 to 400,000 in 1990. Each year throughout this decade, 20,550 programming and 19,000 systems analyst positions are predicted to become available.

One study, "Labor Markets for New Science and Engineering Graduates in Private Industry," performed for the National Science Foundation, is representative of the present employment situation. The study reports the results of a telephone survey of 255 employers that hire computer professionals through campus recruiting. For the years 1980 and 1981, over 40 percent of these firms reported shortages of applicants with bachelor's or master's degrees in computer science, systems analysis, and computer and electrical engineering. Employers found it hardest to find students trained in those areas of the computer industry that have grown most rapidly in recent years. Office machine and computer manufacturers, electronic component manufacturers and computer service companies reported hiring shortfalls. Larger companies, seeking to hire a greater number of computer personnel, felt these shortages most severely.

Employers reported that they were able to fill less than 50 percent of their available computer science positions. The number of job offers extended by employers was significantly lower than their recruitment goals, reflecting a lack of qualified applicants. Nearly 45 percent of employers reported fewer qualified graduates in systems analysis than they sought, although they were able to fill two-thirds of their positions. And companies met only 40 percent of their hiring goals in computer engineering, with many more vacancies than qualified applicants.

We can draw two conclusions from this survey. First, industry's needs for computer science graduates are not being satisfied at present. Second, and perhaps more significant for those considering a career in computer science, is employers' emphasis on their need for *qualified* job candidates. Employers look for quality and expect that quality to be demonstrated by good grades and work experience.

SALARY AND ADVANCEMENT

Appendix A presents the results of a 1983 salary survey conducted by Source EDP. As you can see from these results, computer professionals are financially well-rewarded for their work. A student graduating in 1983 with a B.S. in computer science could expect to receive at least $20,000 in his or her first year of employment. With a master's degree, that figure jumped to around $26,000. Salaries vary with an individual's area of specialization, however. Systems programmers, telecommunications programmers, and data base specialists all start at higher salaries than business or scientific and engineering applications programmers.

Salaries in the computer field generally increase steeply in an employee's first three to five years on the job. After this point, salary increases tend to level off; large increases are related to significant promotions.

Almost without exception, your first position upon graduation will be as a programmer-trainee, junior programmer, or junior programmer/analyst. From this point, your advancement will depend on your abilities and interests, your initiative, and the career goals you set for yourself.

Two paths of advancement are open to you: a technical path and a path leading into management. In the past, most promotions led into management positions. A successful individual would move from programmer to project leader and into higher management. This generally meant, though, that as an employee advanced, the less technical and the more managerial were his or her responsibilities. The result was that people with very good technical qualifications but no interest in management were frustrated by a lack of opportunity.

For the most part, this situation is changing today. Companies have tried to make dual-paths of advancement available to their employees. New job titles and responsibilities have been created in the technical domain. An employee can still advance into management, as before. But successive levels of technical promotions have been created. Texas Instruments' dual track system is one example of this recognition that many computer scientists will be happiest and most productive if technical avenues of promotion exist.

Opportunities for technical promotion are greatest with large computer vendors that have sizable investments in research and development. Opportunities are also found in high-technology industries including telecommunications, aerospace and avionics, and defense.

Within vendor organizations, you can move both vertically and laterally. This means that you might move from a technical position into a position in marketing or technical support, or from one design project to another. Such diversified experience within a single company is a good preparation for advancement into the higher levels of management.

Within user organizations, most promotions lead into management. The chances for technical advancement are few and generally are limited to computer operations. And even here, success and career growth lead to increasing supervisory and managerial responsibilities.

A Note about Equality of Opportunity

Individuals of any sex, race, creed, or ethnic origin can do well in computer science. Because computer science requires mental, not physical, skills, it can be a good choice for those with physical disabilities. People with limited vision, hearing, and mobility have found satisfying positions in the computer field.

SUMMARY

While it is always difficult to predict the future, industry spokesmen generally agree on at least three points. First, as the computer industry continues to mature, programming productivity will become an urgent concern, and the role of the programmer will be altered or even reduced. Manual coding is labor-intensive. That

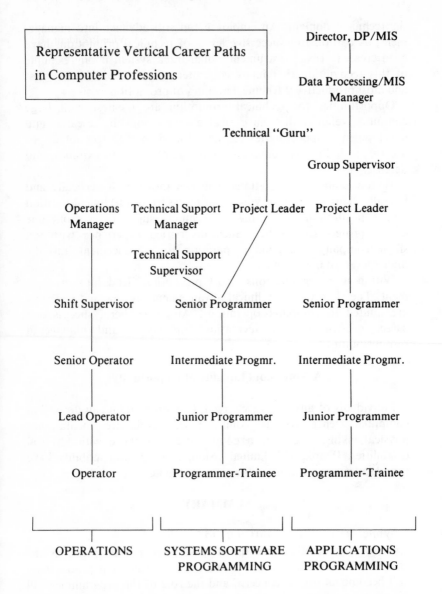

Representative Vertical Career Paths
in Computer Professions

Director, DP/MIS

Data Processing/MIS
Manager

Technical "Guru"

Group Supervisor

Operations
Manager

Technical Support
Manager

Project Leader

Project Leader

Technical Support
Supervisor

Shift Supervisor

Senior Programmer

Senior Programmer

Senior Operator

Intermediate Progmr.

Intermediate Progmr.

Lead Operator

Junior Programmer

Junior Programmer

Operator

Programmer-Trainee

Programmer-Trainee

OPERATIONS

SYSTEMS SOFTWARE
PROGRAMMING

APPLICATIONS
PROGRAMMING

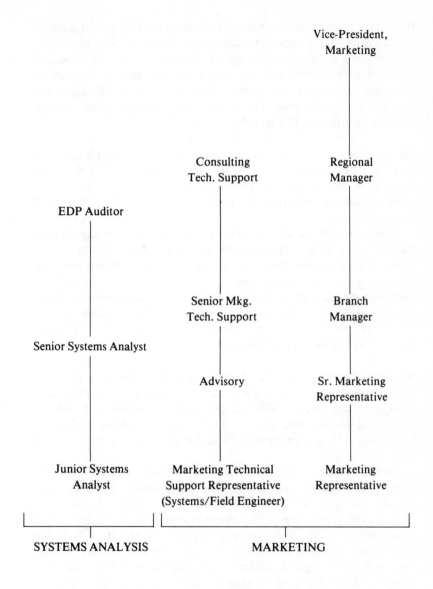

is, it takes many man-hours to write even a small section of code. It has been estimated that, no matter what language they are using, programmers produce an average of eight to ten lines of debugged code a day. As the price of computing has decreased, it becomes increasingly economical to automate the translation of the algorithm into a computer language. This can increase programming productivity to slightly over 30 lines a day.

As the importance of the coder/programmer declines, the role of the systems analyst will become more important. Employers will seek to fill entry-level positions with individuals who can do much more than simply code a program. At the same time, systems analysts will be expected to possess a high level of technical competence.

In addition to automated coding and an emphasis on systems analysis, programmer productivity will be enhanced in other ways. While it may be possible to build software to translate program specifications into the desired code, it is not yet feasible to automate the planning and design states of software projects. Thus, the role of the software engineer, responsible for designing an efficient software system, will come to the fore. And software engineering will be a good career area.

Changes in programming languages and techniques will also improve productivity. Structured programming—dividing a program into self-contained units that can be separately written and debugged—has already affected programming practice. Language design and development, especially of powerful artificial intelligence languages, will help programmers accomplish more in each line of code.

Second, because, in part, of the reduced emphasis on the coder/programmer, competition for entry-level positions will become increasingly tough. We have noted that more and more students are graduating with computer science degrees; this means more and more job candidates are available. Employers will, in the near future, be in a position to be very selective in their hiring. They will look for job candidates with practical experience, not just a degree. Thus, students enrolled in college or university computer science degree programs should do everything they can to gain this experience.

A third and related point is that the possession of a degree in computer science will not guarantee easy access to employment. The quality of the degree, rather than the degree itself, will become increasingly significant. Employers will critically evaluate the education of potential employees. Those who hold degrees from weak programs may find they are less employable than those with degrees from more highly-rated schools.

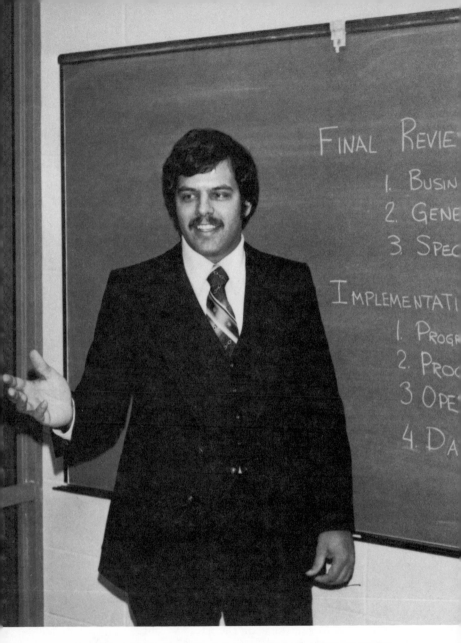

Professional organizations often sponsor courses and seminars to develop
the skills of their members. Photo: Norman N. Noerper.

CHAPTER 9

PROFESSIONAL ORGANIZATIONS

Professional organizations and societies provide a forum for the exchange of information and foster the professional development of their members. Most students will join at least one or two professional organizations in college (usually IEEE Computer Society and/or the Association for Computing Machinery) in order to be able to list their membership on their résumé. It is certainly true that potential employers will see membership in professional organizations as an indication of your serious commitment to computer science. But there are many other, perhaps more important benefits of your membership in these groups. Nearly every professional society listed in the following pages puts out journals, newsletters, or other publications, which you receive as part of your membership. Reading these publications can go a long way toward keeping you up-to-date on technological advances. This is especially important because much of what you learn in school will necessarily be a little out-of-date, if only because of the time it takes to publish a textbook.

You can also keep abreast of developments in computer theory and applications by attending meetings, seminars, and conferences sponsored by professional groups. You can probably learn more in a single day at the National Computer Conference than in several weeks of classroom study. You have the chance to see what vendors are producing, to hear talks on the latest advances in hardware and software, and to learn about recent trends in research and development. Additionally, you can meet and talk with people working in the computer industry. These informal contacts can be very useful in giving you a sense of what is really happening in the computer field. Sometimes, such informal contacts can even lead to employment opportunities.

A very large number of computer-related professional organizations exist today. Listed here are some of the major professional organizations in computing, a selection of special interest groups, and groups that many students might like to join. Most of these groups encourage student membership; some have strong student programs.

AMERICAN FEDERATION OF INFORMATION
    PROCESSING SOCIETIES, INC. (AFIPS)
1815 North Lynn Street, Suite 800
Arlington, VA 22209

The American Federation of Information Processing Societies is an umbrella organization of eleven societies and associations with a primary interest in information processing. AFIPS does not accept individual membership; rather, it represents the members of its constituent societies in matters of common professional concern. AFIPS is the official United States representative to the International Federation for Information Processing, and provides its member organizations with information on actions of the U.S. Congress and federal agencies relevant to computer science and its applications. The AFIPS Press is a major publisher of conference proceedings and other non-periodical publications in the computer field, including research reports and educational materials.

One of the most important events in the computer industry is the National Computer Conference, held each spring under the auspices of AFIPS and its member organizations. People from around the world attend the NCC to see vendor displays of the latest in computer hardware and software and to listen to papers on research and development. Since 1980, AFIPS has also organized an annual Office Automation Conference to bring together individuals and companies concerned with effective development of the office of the future.

AFIPS has prepared a brief pamphlet, "A Look Into Computer Careers," designed to help students explore career options. You can obtain a copy of this pamphlet by writing to AFIPS.

The following eleven organizations form the constituent members of AFIPS. Many of these groups have student memberships; some sponsor activities and competitions in which you may wish to participate.

AMERICAN SOCIETY FOR INFORMATION SCIENCE (ASIS)
1010 Sixteenth Street, N.W.
Washngton, DC 20036

ASIS is concerned with the man-machine interface: the ways in which people can use computer-based information systems and the science and technology behind these systems. ASIS is dedicated to creating, organizing, and transmitting knowledge on all aspects of information and its transfer, including what formerly would have been called library science.

There are regional and student chapters of ASIS throughout the U.S., Canada, and Europe. ASIS maintains a "jobline" of available positions in information science. The jobline is updated weekly and is available free of charge to members and non-members. You can reach the jobline by dialing (202) 659-1737. ASIS has also prepared a brochure on career opportunities in information science. You can obtain this brochure from Society headquarters.

AMERICAN STATISTICAL ASSOCIATION (ASA)
806 Fifteenth Street, N.W.
Washington, DC 20005

The oldest constituent organization in AFIPS, the ASA was founded in 1839, long before the advent of electronic computers. The Association is made up of persons interested in theoretical and/or applied statistics. In addition to its annual meeting in August, the ASA maintains 66 regional chapters in the U.S. and Canada. Student memberships are available.

ASSOCIATION FOR COMPUTATIONAL LINGUISTICS (ACL)

SRI International, EJ278
Menlo Park, CA 94025

The Association for Computational Linguistics, founded in 1962, consists of individuals interested in problems involving computation and natural languages, including voice recognition, natural language processing, and psycholinguistics. Members study the ways in which machines as well as humans process, use, and understand language. The ACL holds an annual conference and publishes the *American Journal of Computational Linguistics*. There are no student memberships in ACL, but the cost of regular membership is modest.

ASSOCIATION FOR COMPUTING MACHINERY (ACM)
11 West 42nd Street
New York, NY 10036

The Association for Computing Machinery stands with the IEEE Computer Society as one of the two major organizations of computer professionals. Founded in 1947, just one year after ENIAC, the first electronic computer, ACM is dedicated to advancing the arts and sciences of computer machinery, techniques, languages, and applications. It encourages the interchange of computer knowledge among professionals and seeks to better inform the general public about computers and computing.

With over 62,000 members and 100 chapters in the U.S. and abroad, ACM plays an important part in the ongoing education and professional development of computer scientists. More than 30 Special Interest Groups within ACM function as independent, smaller organizations of individuals with a common interest in a wide range of topics of theoretical, practical, or social import. Among ACM's many publications are *Communications of the ACM* and the quarterly *Journal of the Association for Computing Machinery*.

ACM has an extremely active student program. You will find ACM Student Chapters at most colleges and universities with computer science departments. Under the direction of faculty advisors, these chapters sponsor educational and social activities. Student contact with members of the computer profession is promoted through the ACM Lectureship Series, which brings outstanding speakers to college campuses.

In addition to chapter activities, ACM holds an annual National Student Programming Contest. Regional winners compete in the finals held at the ACM Computer Science Conference each February. Undergraduate members of ACM can also compete for the George E. Forsythe Award, given annually to the winner of the Student Paper Competition. The winning paper is published in *Communications of the ACM*. Each year, ACM also compiles a guide to graduate assistantships and awards a prize to the author of an outstanding doctoral dissertation.

You can obtain an up-to-date listing of all ACM Student Chapters by writing or telephoning the organization's headquarters in New York. Student membership in this organization is strongly recommended.

ASSOCIATION FOR EDUCATIONAL DATA SYSTEMS (AEDS)
1201 Sixteenth Street, N.W.
Washington, DC 20036

Members of AEDS are interested in the relation of computer technology to modern education, and include educators and computer experts from the U.S., Canada, and overseas. The Association publishes three periodicals: *AEDS Bulletin, AEDS Monitor,* and *AEDS Journal.* It sponsors an annual programming contest for students in junior and senior high school and works in other ways to foster improved knowledge of computers among students and their teachers. Student memberships are available at reasonable rates.

DATA PROCESSING MANAGEMENT ASSOCIATION (DPMA)
505 Busse Highway
Park Ridge, IL 60068

The Data Processing Management Association serves the information processing and computer management community. Its membership comprises systems analysts, data processing managers, and other information processing personnel. Membership in DPMA is granted through local chapters only. Student chapters are active on many college campuses. The DPMA student chapters are highly career-oriented and provide chances for professional contact.

IEEE COMPUTER SOCIETY (IEEE CS)
1109 Spring Street, Suite 300
Silver Spring, MD 20910
West Coast Office
10622 Los Vaqueros Circle
Los Alamitos, CA 90720

The IEEE Computer Society, a constituent society of the Institute of Electrical and Electronics Engineers, Inc., ranks with ACM as one of the two major professional organizations for computer scientists and engineers. With over 80,000 members world-wide and over 100 local chapters, it is also the world's largest organization of computer professionals.

The expressed purpose of the Computer Society is to advance the theory, practice, and applications of computer and information processing science and technology. It encourages the on-going professional education of its members through its sponsorship of more than 60 conferences, workshops, tutorials, and symposia held each year. The IEEE CS is also a major publisher of magazines, journals, and books on computer science. Its publications include five magazines on computer hardware and software design and applications, including the widely-read monthly, *Computer;* three archival journals reporting the latest advances in computer research; and over 500 books on a wide range of computer-related topics. More than 30 technical committees within IEEE CS unite individuals concerned with many special issues in computer science and technology. Members can also subscribe to an electronic mail service.

Because it emphasizes education of computer scientists and engineers, the Computer Society has a strong student program. At the end of 1983, there were over 10,000 student members of IEEE CS and 75 student branch chapters at colleges and universities throughout the U.S.. The Society has also been instrumental in designing criteria to improve, standardize, and recognize by means of ABET accreditation undergraduate programs in computer-related fields.

INSTRUMENT SOCIETY OF AMERICA (ISA)
Box 12277
Research Triangle Park, NC 27709

Members of the ISA share a common interest in the theory, design, manufacture, and use of instruments and controls in science and technology. Society activities cover instrumentation many areas. Senior membership in ISA usually requires a B.S. or engineering degree and six years' work in the instrumentation field. Student memberships, however, are available.

SOCIETY FOR COMPUTER SIMULATION (SCS)
P.O. Box 2228
La Jolla, CA 92038

The SCS is devoted to the use of computers to simulate or model processes, systems, or events. Its members include professionals in science, engineering, mathematics, and computer science. The Society publishes a monthly technical journal, *Simulation*, as well as a series of reports on particular applications of simulation techniques.

SOCIETY FOR INDUSTRIAL AND APPLIED MATHEMATICS (SIAM)
117 South 17th Street
Philadelphia, PA 19103

SIAM exists to further the applications of mathematics in industry and science and to encourage the exchange of ideas among individuals interested in applied mathematics. It publishes nine journals, a newsletter, *SIAM News*, and monographs; holds national meetings; and maintains regional chapters. Student members participate in local university chapters. SIAM sponsors a visiting lectureship program to bring outstanding speakers to campus; it also directs the Institute for Mathematics and Society, which studies the applications of mathematics to major problems of society.

SOCIETY FOR INFORMATION DISPLAY (SID)
654 North Sepulveda Boulevard
Los Angeles, CA 90049

SID encourages advancement in the problems involved in information display. It maintains a central file of information on this subject for the use of its members, sponsors meetings and publications, and is active in defining standards pertaining to information display. Full-time students can join SID at very little cost.

A few of the many other professional organizations and societies related to computer science are listed below.

AMERICAN ASSOCIATION FOR MEDICAL SYSTEMS
    AND INFORMATICS (AAMSI)
Suite 402, 4405 East-West Highway
Bethesda, MD 20814

The AAMSI was formed in 1982 by the merger of the Society for Computer Medicine and the Society for Advanced Medical Systems. Its membership includes physicians, nurses, pharmacists, veterinarians, health care administrators, and computer specialists.

ASSOCIATION FOR SYSTEMS MANAGEMENT (ASM)
24587 Bagley Road
Cleveland, OH 44138

The ASM is the major organization for systems professionals involved in information resource management. The organization encourages the ongoing education of its members through educational courses and seminars and holds an annual conference. Although full membership requires a college degree or experience in the field, ASM does offer student memberships.

ASSOCIATION FOR WOMEN IN COMPUTING (AWC)
407 Hillmoor Drive
Silver Spring, MD 20901

A non-profit organization founded in 1978, AWC membership is made up of over 3,000 men and women interested in encouraging and promoting the success of women in the computer field. The Association has three major goals: 1) to improve communication among women in computing; 2) to improve career development and opportunities for women through workshops, programs, and panel discussions put on by local chapters; and 3) to provide education about computers and computing for women of all ages. At the present time, AWC has 14 chartered local chapters and a number of convening groups in cities throughout the U.S.. Some groups have special educational programs for high school and elementary students; some award scholarships to students in the computer field. AWC also presents the Ada Lovelace award to outstanding women professionals. It actively encourages corporate as well as individual and student memberships.

CANADIAN INFORMATION PROCESSING SOCIETY (CIPS)
243 College Street, 5th Floor
Toronto, Ontario M5T 2Y1
CANADA

CIPS is the largest computer association in Canada, with over 4,000 members, 19 regional sections, and numerous special interest groups. If you are enrolled full-time in a recognized college or university, you may become a student member of CIPS; student members may vote in elections, receive CIPS publications, and are eligible for discounts on registration fees at conferences and seminars sponsored by the Society. Canadian residents should consider joining CIPS.

CENTER FOR COMPUTER LAW
P.O. Box 54308

Los Angeles, CA 90054

The Center for Computer Law is primarily an educational organization aimed at promoting the orderly development of law in the computer, communication, and information fields. It publishes the *Computer/Law Journal*, which covers topics related to computer security law and crime, ownership of software, the use of computers in the legal profession, and the legal implications of computer use in general. The Center has prepared a bibliography of publications relating to computer law.

OPERATIONS RESEARCH SOCIETY OF AMERICA (ORSA)
428 East Preston Street
Baltimore, MD 21202

ORSA is an organization of operations research professionals, managers, teachers, and students interested in scientific methods of decision making that use computers. As of 1982, in addition to regional and technical sections, student sections of ORSA were active at ten universities: Columbia, Cornell, Stanford, Ohio State, UNC at Chapel Hill, NC State at Raleigh, Northwestern, Michigan, UC Berkeley, and Case Western Reserve. ORSA sponsors an annual student paper competition and publishes a comprehensive guide to graduate and undergraduate programs in the field, "Educational Programs in Operations Research."

SOCIETY OF MANUFACTURING ENGINEERS (SME)
1 SME Drive
P.O. Box 930
Dearborn, MI 48121

The Society of Manufacturing Engineers is an international organization with over 70,000 members around the world. It is vitally concerned with student education and sponsors 95 student chapters. SME is the parent organization of three special interest groups, two of which directly concern computers and computing: the Computer and Automated Systems Association (CASA/SME) and Robotics

International (RI/SME).

CASA/SME covers the field of computers and automation in manufacturing. It unites individuals interested in computer-aided design (CAD), computer-aided manufacturing (CAM), and computer-integrated manufacturing (CIM). Its quarterly magazine, *CAD/CAM Technology*, publishes articles of interest to CAD/CAM specialists.

Robotics International was founded in 1980 to encourage information exchange in the rapidly emerging field of robotics. RI's bi-monthly magazine, *Robotics Today*, features information on the latest advances in robot technology and the use of robots in manufacturing operations.

WOMEN IN INFORMATION PROCESSING (WIP)
Suite 9, 1000 Connecticut Avenue, N.W.
Washington, DC 20036

Women in Information Processing is an organization of women in the computer industry, telecommunications, and other fields related to information and data processing. WIP publishes *Parity* magazine. Through a network of meetings and programs, it helps women to find employment and encourages their ongoing professional development. Student memberships in WIP are welcomed.

THE 1983 SALARY SURVEY*

1. Non-Management Positions

(Salary according to length of experience)	Annual Compensation ($000)		
	15th Percentile	Median	85th Percentile
Commercial Programmers and Programmer Analysts			
6 months-1 year	16.2	20.0	25.0
1 year-2 years	18.4	22.9	28.5
2 years-4 years	21.9	26.8	33.9
Over 4 years	25.0	31.3	37.8
Engineering/Scientific Programmers and Programmer Analysts			
6 months-1 year	16.7	20.7	28.4
1 year-2 years	20.1	24.4	31.9
2 years-4 years	24.3	28.8	37.0
Over 4 years	28.6	33.8	43.5

*Reprinted from "1983 Computer Salary Survey and Career Planning Guide," prepared by Source EDP.

Mini/Micro Computer Programmers and Programmer Analysts

6 months-1 year	15.8	20.9	26.8
1 year-2 years	19.1	24.0	30.9
2 years-4 years	21.9	27.7	35.0
Over 4 years	27.3	34.5	42.2

Systems (Software) Programmers

1 year-2 years	21.0	27.3	35.9
2 years-4 years	25.5	31.7	40.3
Over 4 years	31.5	38.1	46.8

Data Base Specialists

1 year-2 years	19.9	26.9	37.6
2 years-4 years	25.5	32.1	39.8
Over 4 years	32.4	40.1	50.3

Tele-Communications Programmers and Programmer Analysts

1 year-2 years	21.8	26.6	32.3
2 years-4 years	24.6	30.7	38.9
Over 4 years	29.7	37.5	46.3

Technical Writers and Editors

6 months-1 year	15.5	20.1	27.1
1 year-2 years	17.1	22.8	30.9
2 years-4 years	21.2	26.7	35.5
Over 4 years	24.3	30.6	37.4

EDP Auditors

1 year-2 years	20.0	23.8	30.6
2 years-4 years	23.5	30.1	36.1
Over 4 years	26.6	38.2	45.8

Senior Analysts, Project Leaders and Consultants			
2 years-4 years	24.0	30.8	38.3
4 years-6 years	28.1	34.7	43.1
Over 6 years	31.5	39.1	56.0

2. Management Positions

(Salary according to size of computer system)	*Annual Compensation ($000)*		
	15th Percentile	*Median*	*85th Percentile*
Technical Services Managers			
Small	26.7	38.2	50.8
Medium	33.5	43.6	54.3
Large	38.2	49.0	62.4
Systems and Programming Managers			
Small	30.0	38.3	43.8
Medium	36.5	44.2	56.1
Large	40.6	49.6	62.4
Operations Managers			
Small	19.7	27.1	32.8
Medium	26.5	34.4	42.7
Large	29.8	40.5	51.3
Information Systems Directors			
Small	30.3	40.6	51.9
Medium	39.7	50.5	63.6
Large	47.5	60.3	89.4

3. Marketing Positions

(Salary according to size of computer system)	Annual Compensation ($000)		
	15th Percentile	*Median*	*85th Percentile*
Marketing Representatives	32.3	43.5	91.5
Marketing Managers	44.0	57.8	106.3
Marketing Technical Support Representatives			
1 year-2 years	17.8	23.9	33.2
2 years-4 years	23.2	30.1	42.3
Over 4 years	28.1	33.6	46.0

SELECTED READINGS

Periodicals
(Trade and commercial)

Byte
Byte Publications, Inc.
70 Main Street
Peterborough, NH 03458
Covers the latest innovations in microcomputer technology.

Computer Systems News
CMP Publications, Inc.
333 East Shore Road
Manhasset, NY 11030

Computerworld
CW Publications
375 Cochituate Road
Framingham, MA 01701
A weekly in newspaper format, *Computerworld* publishes news stories and feature articles. Lots of advertising and an excellent career classified section. Very important.

Datamation
Technical Publishing Company
875 Third Avenue
New York, NY 10022
Major commercial publication for data-processing vendors and users.

Graduating Engineer
McGraw-Hill Publications
1221 Avenue of the
    Americas
New York, NY 10020
Published four times a year. Free to senior and graduate students in engineering and computer science. May be distributed on campus in engineering departments.

Information Systems News
CMP Publications, Inc.
333 East Shore Road
Manhasset, NY 11030

Popular Computing
c/o Subscriptions
P.O. Box 307
Martinsville, NY 08836
Articles on computers, the
computer industry, com-
puter applications, and
personal computing.

Books

Dertouzos, Michael L. and
Joel Moses, eds. *The Computer Age: A Twenty-Year
View*. Cambridge, MA:
The MIT Press, 1979. A
collection of articles on the
impact of computers on
society.

*Encyclopedia of Computer
Science and Engineering*.
Second edition. New York:
Van Nostrand Reinhold
Company, 1983. Excellent
reference work on com-
puters and computer
science.

Feigenbaum, Edward A.
and Pamela McCorduck.
The Fifth Generation.
Reading, MA: Addison-
Wesly Publishing Com-
pany, 1983. Relatively ac-
cessible account of current
work in artificial
intelligence.

Kidder, Tracy. *The Soul of
a New Machine*. Boston:
Little, Brown and Co.,
1981. This 1982 Pulitzer
Prize-winner tells the story
of the project team designing Data General's Eclipse
computer. A good descrip-
tion of the daily work of
computer scientists.
Available in paperback
from Avon.

Noerper, Norman N. *Op-
portunities in Data Proc-
essing*. Lincolnwood, IL:
VGM Career Horizons,
1984.

Shelly, Gary B. and
Thomas J. Cashman. *In-
troduction to Computers
and Data Processing*.
Fullerton, CA: Anaheim
Publishing Company,
1980. A readable general
introduction.

VGM CAREER HORIZONS SERIES

CAREER PLANNING

How To Land A Better Job
Life Plan
Planning Your College
  Education
Planning Your Military Career

SURVIVAL GUIDES

High School Survival Guide
College Survival Guide

OPPORTUNITIES IN

*Available in both
paperback and hardbound
editions*
Accounting
Acting
Advertising
Airline Careers
Animal and Pet Care
Appraising Valuation Science
Architecture
Automotive Service
Banking
Beauty Culture
Biological Sciences
Book Publishing
Broadcasting
Building Construction
  Trades
Cable Television
Carpentry
Chemical Engineering
Chemistry
Chiropractic Health Care
Civil Engineering
Computer Science
Counseling & Guidance
Dance
Data Processing
Dental Care

Drafting
Electrical Trades
Electronic and Electrical
  Engineering
Energy Careers
Engineering Technology
Environmental Careers
Fashion
Film
Fire Protection Services
Food Services
Foreign Language Careers
Forestry
Free Lance Writing
Government Service
Graphic Communications
Health and
  Medical Careers
Hospital Administration
Hotel & Motel Management
Industrial Design
Interior Design
Journalism
Landscape Architecture
Law Careers
Law Enforcement and
  Criminal Justice
Library and Information
  Science
Machine Shop Trades
Magazine Publishing
Management
Marine & Maritime
Materials Science
Mechanical Engineering
Modeling
Music
Nursing
Occupational Therapy
Office Occupations
Opticianry
Optometry
Packaging Science

Paralegal Careers
Paramedical Careers
Personnel Management
Pharmacy
Photography
Physical Therapy
Podiatric Medicine
Psychiatry
Psychology
Public Relations
Real Estate
Recreation and Leisure
Refrigeration and
  Air Conditioning
Religious Service
Sales & Marketing
Secretarial Careers
Securities Industry
Sports & Athletics
Sports Medicine
Teaching
Technical
  Communications
Telecommunications
Theatrical Design
  & Production
Transportation
Travel Careers
Veterinary Medicine
Writing Careers

WOMEN IN

*Available in both
paperback and
hardbound editions*
Communications
Engineering
Finance
Government
Management
Science
Their Own Business

VGM Career Horizons

A Division of National Textbook Company
4255 West Touhy Avenue
Lincolnwood, Illinois 60646-1975 U.S.A.

DATE DUE

FEB 3			
MAR 28			
Feb 14			
30 505 JOSTEN'S